Soups, Pasta and Rice Dishes

Colour Library of Step by Step Cookery

Soups, Pasta and Rice Dishes

Translated and adapted by Marie-Christine Comte
With an introduction by Gill Edden

ORBIS BOOKS·LONDON

Contents

Photographs by Paola Martini
Drawings by Walter Bloor and David Higham, courtesy of David Mellor-Ironmonger, London
Recipes adapted from l'Unil-It, SpA
ISBN 0 85613 170 9

Foreword

Rice, pasta and soups – these are some of the world's basic foods. Both rice and pasta are basic grain products that comprise the staple diet of their countries of origin, while soup has for centuries been the main meal of mid-European peasants. Basic as these foods are, there is no reason why they cannot also take their place on an elegant dinner table for, well prepared and presented, they can make delightful dishes. Take the trouble to learn to cook them properly and you will have the makings of many a fine repast.

The Colour Library of Step by Step Cookery will cover the whole range of good cooking. Each book is complete in itself and together they take you from the start of a meal to the end. In them we describe the preparation of dishes with the greatest care and include plenty of detailed information about the foods used, their nutritional values and how to make the best of them. You will find few short cuts – our recipes are based mainly on traditional French and Italian cooking – but anyone who takes the trouble to follow our methods will have earned a right to the prestige that goes with 'keeping a good table'.

Each volume in the series contains a glossary of the special cooking terms used. In the course of the series we shall cover everything you need to know about meal planning, garnishes, herbs and spices and the preparation of all kinds of foods. We haven't neglected drinks and preserving is also included. The basis of good cooking is an international tradition. It is a skill that is fundamental to home-making and to successful entertaining alike.

Glossary

Al dente
Italian expression meaning just tender but not soft ('to the tooth'). To test, press the food (usually pasta or rice) with the thumb nail; it should cut cleanly.

Anchovy
Canned anchovies need desalting before use. Soak or wash them very thoroughly in water or milk and dry on absorbent paper. Scrape them to remove all the scales and cut into small fillets or use according to the recipe.

Bain-marie
Literally a 'water bath'. Consists of a pan of hot water in which another pan or pans may be stood for cooking. Used for cooking sauces and custards that may curdle if cooked too quickly over direct heat, and for keeping sauces warm without further cooking.

Bard, to
To cover a joint of meat or the breast of a bird with fat or fat bacon to prevent it drying out during cooking.

Beef marrow
The bones, particularly the shank bones of a bullock, are filled with a softish substance called marrow. When bones are cooked for stock it is the marrow which helps to make a good jelly. The marrow can also be scooped out of the bone and used as a nourishing ingredient in dishes.

Croûtons
Small pieces of bread or potato, toasted or fried and used as a garnish for a hot meat dish or more commonly a soup.

Curry
A savoury dish of Eastern, and particularly Indian, origin. It is highly flavoured with a mixture of spices. In the west the spices for a basic curry are sold ready ground and mixed, as curry powder; the main ingredients are pepper, cayenne, cloves, mace, coriander, turmeric, cumin, ginger, cardamom and fenugreek.

Gratiné, to
To brown the top of a dish. The food is generally sprinkled with breadcrumbs, butter and sometimes grated cheese, then placed in a hot oven or under a preheated grill until brown. A fireproof dish with handles at either end is known as a gratin dish.

Julienne strips
Small matchstick shapes of vegetable, meat or other food, usually for use as a garnish.

Parboil, to
To cook partly, by boiling, prior to completing cooking by some other method. This is to ensure the food is soft right to the centre.

Polenta
Corn or maize meal generally served as an accompaniment, or used in bread, cakes and gnocchi. Semolina can sometimes be used as a substitute.

Roux
A cooked mixture of fat and flour, which forms the base of many sauces.

Sauté, to
To brown food quickly in butter or oil and butter. Sometimes cooking is finished in the sauce that is made with the food in the sauté pan.

Scald, to
To heat almost to boiling point.

Timbale
A high sided round mould for meat or fish creams. A dish served 'en timbale' is one piled up in a circle.

Tomatoes
To peel tomatoes, first dip them in boiling water for 10–12 seconds to loosen the skin. Alternatively, hold the tomato on a fork in the flame of a gas jet, turning it until the skin is scorched all over; it will then peel easily.

Rice

The staple food of about half the human race, rice thrives in hot moist climates such as in India, China, Japan, Indonesia and parts of the USA. Until recently it was somewhat despised in European cooking, particularly in France, but this was chiefly due to a lack of understanding of how best to cook it – there is nothing worse than soggy rice, with all the grains stuck together and broken; the pleasures of eating well-cooked rice, all the grains whole and separate, are now more appreciated and rice is taking its place alongside potatoes as one of our main starch foods.

The peoples who rely on rice for their principal nourishment always use it unpolished because most of its vitamin B content (rice's chief nutritive value) lies just under the husk. Polished rice has almost all its nutritive value removed. If these peoples were to substitute polished rice in their diet they would start to contract beriberi; it was the study of this disease which first led scientists to the theory of vitamins, which now plays a large part in nutritional sciences.

Types of Rice

There are three main types of white rice used in the West: the long, medium and round grain rice. The shorter grained Carolina rice is used chiefly for desserts and long grained Patna rice for boiling and serving with savoury dishes. Remember that 'Carolina' and 'Patna' are used to identify types of rice, not necessarily to indicate the place of origin. As the round grain variety absorbs most liquid – and medium grain only slightly less – these types are good to use for pilaffs and puddings where the liquid adds to the general flavour of the dish.

Brown rice, which is the unpolished white grain, is richer in vitamins, and needs to be well cooked – for about 35 minutes in boiling water.

Wild rice, being the seeds of a grass, is a different plant altogether. It has a distinctive nutty flavour and firm texture, and takes longer to cook than white rice.

Ground rice and rice flour are also used for making puddings, moulds and cakes. For use with cakes, however, rice flour has to be mixed with wheat flour as alone it does not give a sufficiently elastic dough to produce a good textured cake.

Most of us associate rice pudding with the nursery, but this is simply because a rice and milk baked pudding is the easiest way of using the grain to produce a palatable and nourishing dish. But there are several classic dessert dishes based on rice that are worthy of any dinner table. The chief of these is Riz à l'Impératrice, and there are many variations.

Rice for savoury dishes demands quite a different treatment. More often than not this is served as plain boiled rice to accompany spicy meat dishes such as curry, where its bland, neutral flavour makes an ideal background for hot spices. A pilaff, however, can be a dish in itself, including a variety of ingredients, or be highly flavoured and served with other dishes.

Risottos are best made with unwashed round grain rice (pick this over well to remove any grains with the husks left on), and a really strong veal or chicken stock. Whereas the rice in a cooked pilaff is traditionally fluffy and dry, that of an Italian-style risotto should be firm yet creamy.

The Iranians like their rice very dry, even with a brown undercrust, while most Orientals prefer it moist so as to pick it up easily with chopsticks.

How to Cook Rice

The way the Indians cook their rice is the best from the nutritional point of view. The rice is poured lightly into a pan containing just enough boiling salted water to last the duration of the cooking. When cooking is complete all the water should have been absorbed by the rice, leaving it tender, dry and fluffy. The difficulty with this method is of course judging the exact amount of water required, though some brands of rice carry instructions for this method on the package, indicating just the amount of water needed. The advantage is that none of the valuable vitamins are thrown away with the cooking water.

The second method demands less precision. A large quantity of water is brought to the boil, the rice is poured in and cooked until *al dente*, just tender (not more than 12 minutes); the water is then drained off and if necessary the rice may be rinsed of the excess starch with a cup of hot water. The rice must be drained thoroughly in a colander, preferably over a low heat. To reheat rice cooked in this way, spoon it into a buttered ovenproof dish, cover the rice with foil and reheat in a moderate oven for about 30 minutes. The chief points to remember with either of these methods are the same:

1. The water must be boiling when the rice is added.
2. The rice should be 'rained' lightly into the water so that it never stops boiling.
3. The rice should never be stirred.
4. The water must be kept boiling throughout cooking, as this keeps the grains moving, preventing them sticking to each other and the pan.
5. Never overcook rice; there is no way of recovering it once it becomes too soft. It should be cooked until it is just *al dente* and no more.

An alternative method of cooking rice, favoured with Chinese food, is by frying. The rice is boiled first, or sometimes steamed, then fried quickly in hot oil, with savoury additions.

Pasta

Chiefly an Italian product, pasta is made from a hard wheat grain called durum wheat, mixed with water and flavoured with oil and salt. It may be flavoured additionally with eggs and spices such as turmeric or dyed with vegetable colouring. There are a number of traditional variations on the basic product but few people outside Italy now make their own pasta as it is readily available in grocery stores, and is relatively cheap. As far as food value is concerned, 4 oz (115 g) pasta is the equivalent of about 5 oz (150 g) bread.

Apart from the variations in consistency, colour and flavouring, there are traditional variations in shape and it is by these that the different pasta products are known. The most common varieties are:

Spaghetti Made as long, round strands which when cooked expand to about $\frac{1}{8}$ inch diameter. Sold in lengths of 12–18 inches. Serve as a starter or main dish.

Macaroni Similar to spaghetti but tubular. The diameter of the tube is slightly larger than that of spaghetti. This is traditionally sold in long strands, but can also be bought cut into short lengths of 1–2 inches. Serve as spaghetti.

Noodles This egg pasta comes in fine, long strands, fine strands cut into short lengths, or small decorative shapes such as shells, alphabet shapes, stars etc. It is often used as a garnish for soups.

Ravioli Small envelopes of pasta containing a stuffing of meat or vegetable. Serve as starter or main dish.

Cannelloni Large tubes of pasta about 1 inch in diameter, served with a meat filling and a rich sauce as a starter or main dish.

Lasagne Squares of pasta, usually measuring about 4–5 inches. Green spinach colouring is common in this type. Lasagne is served in a large baking dish, layered with meat and cheese sauces.

Other pasta comes in long flat strands and all sorts of shapes and sizes. Some of the better known names not already mentioned are vermicelli, crescioni, ditalini, strichetti, tagliatelli, tortellini.

Gnocchi are also classed as pasta, but are slightly different from the other types in that they are nearly always made at home. French gnocchi are made like a choux paste, with water or milk, flour, butter and eggs, but poached instead of baked (though they may be baked after poaching, to give them a good colour). Italian gnocchi, or gnocchi alla Romana, are made of polenta or maize meal, or if this is not available a coarse semolina may be substituted. The meal is mixed with milk, flavoured with cheese and either baked or boiled. For frying, Italian gnocchi are sometimes coated with egg and breadcrumbs. The third type of gnocchi is potato gnocchi, made from freshly boiled and mashed potato mixed with flour; this is shaped into rolls or triangles and poached. Potato gnocchi vary considerably in quality because different types of potato require the addition of different quantities of flour, and this is a matter of experience. Small gnocchi are sometimes called 'gnocchetti'.

How to Cook Pasta

The basic method is the same for all types, though the cooking time will vary according to the thickness of the pasta. As with rice, the pasta goes into a large pan of fast boiling, salted water. The longer shapes such as spaghetti are gently coiled round the pan as they soften, never broken up. The water is then brought back to the boil and allowed to simmer (*not* fast boil this time) until the pasta is *al dente*. The following is a rough guide to cooking times:

Macaroni 15 minutes
Spaghetti, ravioli, noodles 12 minutes
Vermicelli 7–10 minutes

When it is cooked, turn the pasta into a colander, drain it and rinse with a cup of hot water. Rinse out the cooking pan, put in it a large knob of butter and return the pasta to the pan. Season it well with freshly ground black pepper and toss it until it is well coated and glistening with the butter or serve it according to whatever recipe you are following.

Most pasta recipes take their names from the sauce that accompanies them, and many sauces can be used with the various types of pasta. The most common ingredients for the sauces are tomatoes, onions, mushrooms and Parmesan cheese. Chicken livers and other meats also make their appearance, but in lesser quantities.

How to Serve Pasta

All pasta is served either as a hot hors d'oeuvre or as a main dish, depending on the quantity served. Remember that if you serve pasta as a starter, it should be in small quantities and be followed by something quite light. The success of a pasta dish depends not only on how well the pasta itself is cooked, but also on the sauce served with it. In Italy, pasta is often served simply tossed in butter and sprinkled with grated Parmesan cheese; this tends to be rather dull for unaccustomed palates, though, and outside Italy a more interesting sauce is appreciated. Alternatively, of course, pasta may accompany any meat dish (not a roast) instead of potatoes.

Whenever you serve it, remember that pasta is very filling and will not need a starchy vegetable to accompany it – tomatoes are the most obvious choice.

Garnishes

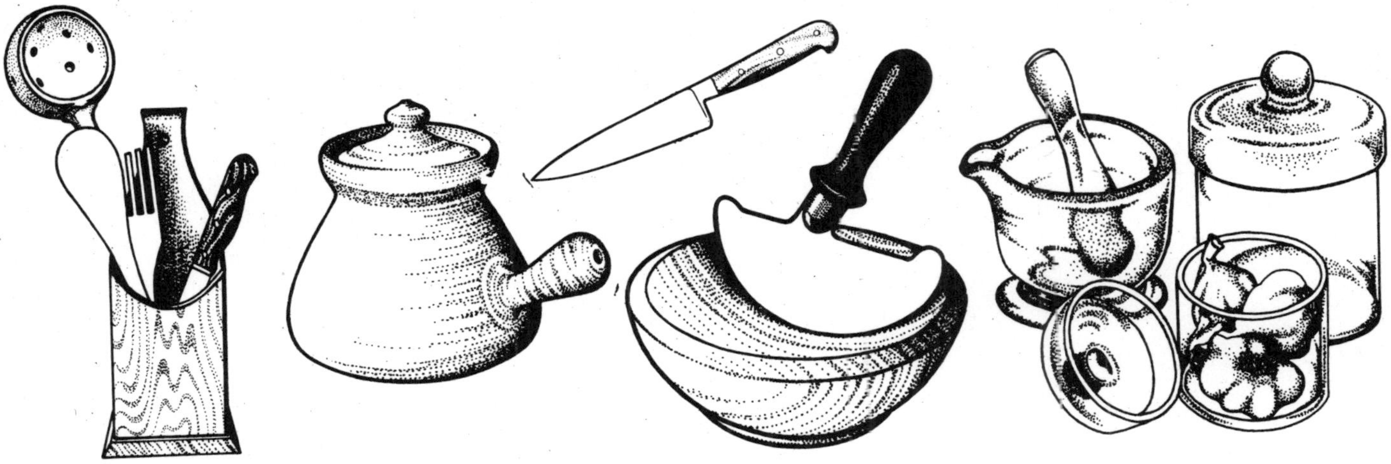

A garnish improves both the look and the flavour of a dish. It must always be edible and may either be very simple, such as chopped herbs scattered over before serving, or something more elaborate such as the following:

Croûtons Small fancy shapes of bread (toasted or fried) or potato (fried). The most common shape is a simple cube, about $\frac{1}{4}$–$\frac{1}{2}$ inch thick, but the croûtons may be triangles, crescents or more elaborate shapes cut with a biscuit cutter. Scatter on top of soup, or use slightly larger croûtons with meat dishes.

Cheese croûtes Slightly larger croûtons of bread may be scattered with grated cheese and baked in a moderate oven. Float on top of a thick vegetable soup, or overlap round the edge of a savoury dish.

Fleurons Puff pastry makes an attractive garnish for meat and poultry dishes if rolled out to about $\frac{1}{4}$ inch thick and cut into small fancy shapes, a crescent being the traditional one. Place the pastry shapes on a baking sheet, brush the tops lightly with beaten egg to glaze them and bake in a hot oven for about 10 minutes, until risen and golden brown.

Breadcrumbs Used in several forms as garnishes. They can be freshly grated, in which case they give a lightly coloured, softish topping or coating. Dried breadcrumbs give a darker, drier finish.

To make dried breadcrumbs, spread fresh crumbs on baking sheets and dry in a very low oven or some other warm place; work them in the blender or rub them through a sieve to make them an even size and store when cool in an airtight jar.

To make buttered breadcrumbs, melt 1 oz (30 g) butter and add 1 lb (500 g) fresh white crumbs. Allow them to absorb the fat, turning the mixture occasionally with a fork, then spread them out on baking sheets (as for dried breadcrumbs) and dry them in a low oven. These can be stored as for dried breadcrumbs and used for gratin dishes.

Vegetable Shapes

Most root vegetables can be sliced and cut into fancy shapes with a biscuit cutter. Beetroot and carrot make the most colourful garnishes. Potato, parsnip etc should be sautéed.

Julienne strips Cut thin strips of raw vegetable, about $1\frac{1}{4}$–$1\frac{1}{2}$ inches long, by about $\frac{1}{8}$ inch thick. Cook lightly if required, or use raw.

Turned mushrooms Cut tiny triangular fillets from the edges of the caps of button mushrooms to notch them all the way round, and then sauté the caps in butter.

Crimped cucumber Cucumber and other vegetables with a dark skin and light flesh can be prepared this way. Run the prongs of a fork down the whole vegetable, to remove strips of skin. Repeat all the way round. Then cut the cucumber into slices a little thicker than normal, so that the remaining strips of dark skin show.

Gherkin fans These make an ideal garnish for a mixed hors d'oeuvre tray. Slice the gherkin lengthwise almost to the base but without cutting through, then open out the slices into a fan.

Radish roses Cut a narrow slice from the root end of each radish, then cut thin petals from stem to root. Drop the radishes into iced water until the petals open out.

Celery curls Cut strips of celery about $\frac{1}{2}$ inch wide and 2 inches long. Slit both ends in narrow strips almost to the centre, but do not join the slits. Leave the celery in iced water until the ends curl.

Spring onions Slit down the stems in fine strips and leave in iced water until the ends curl.

Carrot curls Scrape raw carrots and slice them lengthwise using a potato peeler, so that the slices are paper thin. Roll up the strips and fasten them with a cocktail stick. Drop them in iced water and they will adopt the curl and the stick can be taken out.

Soups

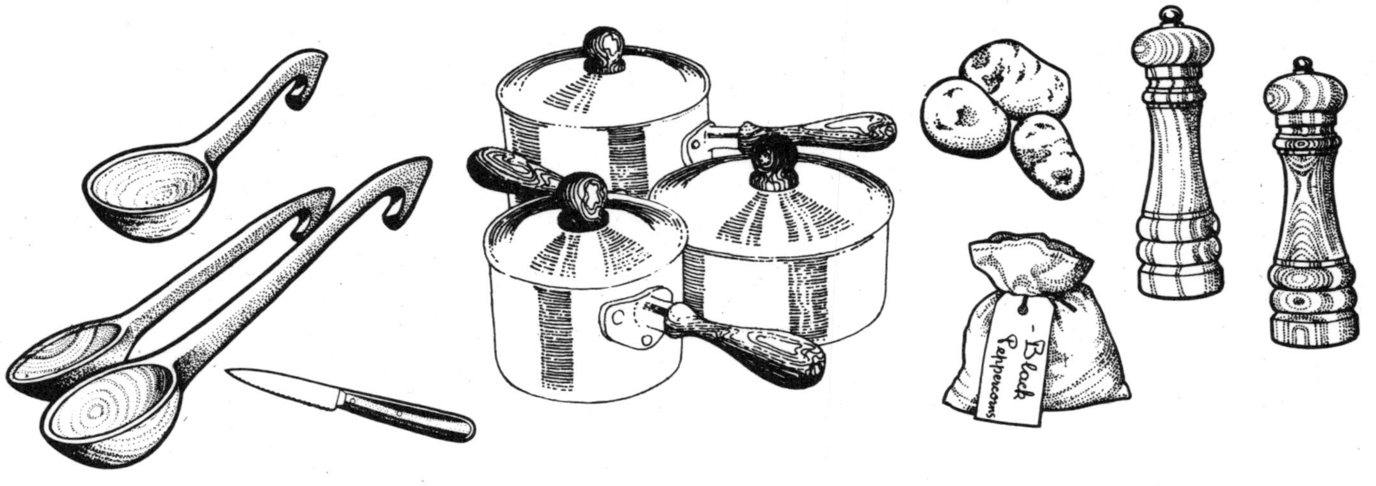

There are still many parts of the world where soup, perhaps alongside a loaf of bread and a jug of wine, is synonymous with the word food. In Germany and Austria and other mid-European countries there are still many families whose main meal of the day goes under the simple name of soup. In Vienna, one of the traditional centres of good cooking, any first class hotel will serve a three or four course meal starting with soup. In less civilized parts of the world, where packages and cans predominate in the kitchen cupboard, the ability and willingness to make a good home-made soup is perhaps the one single item that divides the real cooks from the rest.

Soup making is really not difficult or time consuming, as many people seem to imagine. True, the stock bones must cook for a long while, but that doesn't mean the cook has to be watching them, and the final process of adding vegetables or other ingredients takes no time at all. Finally, if you have a blender, that friend of all modern cooks, purée and cream soups come within your reach with only the slightest exertion on your part.

Hot tasty soups can make an appetizing starter to a meal, or a meal on their own. Made in large quantities, they will keep in the refrigerator for 3–4 days provided they do not contain cream, and they are ideal subjects for home freezing. In fact it pays always to make large quantities of soup. Serve it either with bread and cheese for a quick and nourishing lunch, or as a starter to the main meal for all the family.

A blender isn't essential for soup making, but it is the ideal accessory for making smooth, creamy purées. If you don't have a blender, buy a Mouli sieve; this will give you a little more work but the results will be good just the same. Even if you do have a blender, a sieve will still be necessary for some soups to remove tiny hard lumps such as tomato seeds. If you sieve after blending it will be that much easier.

The basis of all good soups is a stock. Once in a while, of course, we all use a stock cube, but beware of doing this too often; cube stock has a distinctive flavour all of its own and is instantly recognizable. It is very salty and also lacks the characteristic jellied quality of the real bone stock.

Consommé

There are two basic types of soup – clear and thick. A clear soup is known as a consommé. It consists of a good stock enriched still further with meat, poultry or game. The meat is not served with the soup, but may be served separately if you wish. The best consommés are clarified through a filter of egg white before serving; the white of an egg is whisked into the boiling liquid then allowed to set into a crust, the egg white collects into its mass many of the tiny particles of meat and herbs that have remained in the liquid after ordinary straining. As a final clarification the filter is tipped gently on to a scalded cloth and the consommé is strained right through the filter and cloth into a bowl. By this time the liquid should be positively sparkling – if not the process can be repeated.

Garnishes for Consommé

There are literally hundreds of possible garnishes for a consommé, many of them very specific and traditional. In the ordinary way a consommé may be served with a little vermicelli or shell pasta in it, with a handful of rice in each serving, or with julienne strips of vegetables – the latter garnish is particularly attractive since it adds colour to the soup. Alternatively you can add some of the meat used to make the soup, cut into julienne strips. Another common way to serve a consommé, known as Stracciatella, and one that enriches it as a family dish is to whip a little beaten egg into the boiling soup; the heat will cook the egg in strands.

Apart from these substantial garnishes, there are many that simply add a little colour to the consommé – croûtons of fried bread or potato for instance, a sprinkling of chopped parsley or fresh tarragon or chervil. Some consommés, especially those garnished with pasta, are served with grated Parmesan cheese to sprinkle on top.

Thick Soups

These may be a simple purée of vegetables in stock. If the vegetable contains a certain amount of starch, no extra thickening will be necessary; if a vegetable is used that contains little starch, another one is often added to provide the thickening – leek and potato is a common mixture that illustrates this principle. Alternatively, cream soups may be based on a béchamel sauce, to which the flavouring ingredient and extra stock are added, or they may be thickened with a liaison. The most common liaison is a mixture of egg yolks and cream.

Liaisons

The yolks and cream are worked together, a little of the hot soup is blended in and then the liaison is stirred gradually into the main bulk of the soup. Reheat after adding the liaison, stirring continually, but take care not to boil it or it will curdle. This gives a particularly rich soup, but remember, it does not keep like other soups so do not try to store and reheat it. If you have made a large quantity of soup that you want to thicken this way, thicken only that portion that you intend to use each time, and store the rest unthickened. Simpler but less rich liaisons are arrowroot and beurre manié.

To thicken a soup with arrowroot, simply blend a teaspoon of arrowroot with a couple of tablespoons of water and stir the mixture slowly into the hot soup, off the heat. Bring the soup back to the boil, stirring all the time, to cook the arrowroot, then it is ready to serve. This soup can be stored and reheated for several days.

For beurre manié, work together a mixture of flour and butter, using twice as much butter as flour. Add the beurre manié to the soup in small pieces, stirring it in until the soup is sufficiently thick. This can also be stored and reheated without problems arising.

Other Types of Soup

Not all soups are served hot. Summer entertaining calls for a selection of soups to be served chilled. A good clarified consommé (that will of course turn to jelly when chilled) is perhaps the most common and most elegant, but many of the cream soups are just as good cold as hot.

Some vegetable soups fall mid-way between thick and clear. These are the soups like minestrone, where there are so many vegetables in the soup that the basic stock can hardly be seen, but the vegetables are not puréed and there is no liaison added. To make a more substantial soup it is also common to add small meatballs or dumplings.

Menu Planning

Nutritional considerations are the most important for family meals, for it is our daily intake of a balanced diet that keeps us healthy or otherwise, and the occasional party meal will make little difference. With guests, however, the emphasis turns more to the balance of flavours and textures – even the colours of different foods, and of course the planning of advance preparation becomes all important.

No guest likes to be aware of the hostess running to the kitchen every few minutes, or carefully watching the clock, so party menus must be chosen that need little last minute attention, or only one dish that has to be cooked after the guests have arrived.

For example, if your main dish must be carefully timed, start with a pâté made several days in advance and serve with crusty French bread. With grills you can serve baked jacket potatoes that will wait happily in the oven without spoiling, and a tossed salad. For dessert a cold soufflé or an iced dessert will ensure that you are not worrying in case it spoils with waiting. More ambitious cooks will not be satisfied with such simple menus every time – and dinner parties would be very dull if they were – but the principle remains the same of two prepared courses to one needing last minute attention.

Next in importance is the balance of textures. Many hostesses make the mistake of believing that a party is the time to produce all their favourite, richest dishes. So you are served with a lobster bisque, veal à la crème and chocolate mousse with whipped cream – so rich and creamy that few guests appreciate the whole meal. How much better to follow the lobster bisque with a light dish of grilled sole or sautéed veal cutlets, or precede the veal à la crème by something fresh and appetizing such as melon cocktail or a salad of green beans and tomatoes. Chocolate mousse is a good dinner party choice, both popular and easy to prepare in advance, but it should only follow a light menu, and then with a crisp biscuit to help offset its richness.

Pasta dishes often present difficulties for dinner-party menus. They can be so filling that it is a problem to decide what to serve with them. The answer is almost always fresh salads and fruit dishes. The typical Italian choice to precede a main course of lasagne might be melon with a slice of very thinly cut prosciutto, and to follow some fresh, ripe peaches in wine.

If served as a first course, the pasta portions should be small. With cannelloni or spaghetti, follow with small neck cutlets of young lamb, grilled or sautéed, and accompany with fresh green vegetables, zucchini or tomatoes. For dessert, stay on the light side with a cream or water ice, or a sherbet.

Substantial dishes made with pasta and rice are ideal for informal supper parties. Try a dish of richly buttered or peppered noodles with a spicy sauce or a bowl full of tasty meatballs, or a paella. With either menu, the guests need no more equipment than a plate or bowl and a fork.

Catering Quantities

Family Catering

(Approximate quantities per person per meal)

Meat	
with bone	4–6 oz (115–175 g)
boneless	3–4 oz (90–115 g)
for made-up dishes	2–3 oz (60–90 g)
Fish	
with a lot of bone	6–7 oz (175–200 g)
filleted	3–4 oz (90–115 g)
for made-up dishes	2–3 oz (60–90 g)
Vegetables	
(weight unprepared)	
Broad beans	8–12 oz (225–340 g)
Butter beans	2 oz (60 g)
Haricot beans	2 oz (60 g)
Runnerbeans	6 oz (175 g)
Beet (beetroot)	4–6 oz (115–175 g)
Brussels sprouts	6 oz (175 g)
Cabbage	6–8 oz (175–225 g)
Carrots	4–6 oz (115–175 g)
Celeriac	4–6 oz (115–175 g)
Celery	¼ of a large head
Curly kale	6–8 oz (115–225 g)
Greens (spring)	8 oz (225 g)
Onions (served alone)	6 oz (175 g)
Parsnips	6 oz (175 g)
Peas	8 oz (225 g)
Potatoes	6–8 oz (175–225 g)
Rutabaga	8 oz (225 g)
Sea kale	4 oz (115 g)
Spinach	8–12 oz (225–340 g)
Turnips	8 oz (225 g)
Cereals	
Rice or pasta	1–1½ oz (30–45 g)
Soup	¼ pint (150 ml)
Sauces and Gravies	2 fl oz (75 ml)

Party Catering

Sandwiches
2 lb (1 kg) loaf gives 20–24 slices, using ¼ lb (115 g) butter. Allow 1 round of sandwiches per person.

Sandwich fillings
For a 2 lb (1 kg) loaf allow one of the following: 1 lb (500 g) tomatoes, 1 cucumber, 12 oz (340 g) cooked and sliced ham, 3 cans sardines, or 3 scrambled eggs.

Cold meat, poultry, etc.
Sliced and without bone – 2 oz (60 g) per person.

Turkey
14 lb (6½ kg) turkey will serve about 25 people (cold with salads).

Lobster
A good sized lobster gives 3–5 portions (cold with salads).

Sausage rolls
1½ lb (750 g) pastry (i.e. made with 1½ lb/750 g flour, etc.), and 2 lb (1 kg) sausages give about 50 rolls.

Vol-au-vent
1½ lb (750 g) puff pastry makes about 75 small vol-au-vent cases.

Lettuce
1 large lettuce serves 6–8 people.

Tea
For 100 people allow about 5 gallons (22 l) of tea, using 3 oz (90 g) tea per gallon (4½ l) of water. Allow 6–8 pints (3–4½ l) milk, 2 lb (1 kg) sugar.

Coffee
For 100 people allow about 4 gallons (18 l). Use 3 gallons (13 l) water and 1 gallon (4½ l) milk. The quantity of coffee depends on variety, but use 2–3 oz (60–90 g) per gallon (4½ l) for instant coffee.

Wine
1 bottle gives 6 glasses (3¾ fl oz/130 ml).

Champagne
1 bottle gives 5 glasses.

Sherry
1 bottle gives 16 glasses (2½ fl oz/90 ml).

Spirits
1 quart or litre bottle gives from 20–32 single measures.

Comparative Measurements

Metric Working Equivalents

For cooks using these recipes the following working equivalents form a useful guide for when provisions are available only in metric weights.

Ounce/Gram (g)	Working Equivalent
1 oz = 28·35 g	30 g
2 oz = 56·7 g	60 g
4 oz = 113·4 g	115 g
8 oz = 226·8 g	225 g
12 oz = 340·2 g	340 g
16 oz/1 lb = 453·6 g	500 g
2 lb = 907·2 g	1000 g/ 1 kilogram (kg)

Oven Temperatures Guide

Centigrade	Fahrenheit	Gas
250°		
	475°	9
Very hot		
	450°	8
225°		
	425°	7
Hot		
	400°	6
200°		
Moderate to moderately hot	375°	5
175°	350°	4
Moderately slow	325°	3
150°		
	300°	2
Slow	275°	1
125°		
	250°	½
Very slow		
	225°	¼
100°		
	200°	

Boiling point	100 °C	212 °F
Simmering	96 °C	205 °F
Tepid	37 °C	98 °F
Freezing	0 °C	32 °F

Liquid Equivalents

US	British	Metric
4½ cups, or 1 quart 2 oz	1¾ pints	1 litre
2 cups, or 1 pint, or 16 fl oz (generous)	¾ pint, or 15 fl oz (generous)	½ litre (demi-litre), or 426 ml
½ cup, or ¼ pint, or 4 fl oz (scant)	3–4 oz	1 dl, or 142 ml

US pint = 16 fl oz
US cup = ½ pint/8 fl oz
British (Imperial) pint = 20 fl oz
British Standard cup = ½ pint/10 fl oz

1 decilitre (dl) = 1/10 litre
1 centilitre (cl) = 1/100 litre
1 millilitre (ml) = 1/1000 litre

Oven Temperatures These are not constant throughout the oven area. The thermostat measures the degree of heat in the middle of the oven, but the differential between this reading and those at the top and bottom (the hottest area is at the top in most ovens) may be as much as 25°F. This should be taken into account in positioning shelves.

Foods which need slow cooking are best placed towards the bottom of the oven while foods with leavening agents need to be placed in the hottest part of the oven so as to release the carbon dioxide and burst the starch grains.

Care should be taken in positioning dishes to avoid contact with burners or elements and when baking cakes, for instance, to allow sufficient room for the heat to circulate around the baking tins.

Measuring Guide Dry ingredients should be measured before they are sifted. The measuring utensil should be filled to the point of overflowing and the top levelled off by drawing a knife over the surface.

Fats can be quickly and easily measured by displacement. To measure ¾ cup of fat, fill a measuring cup ¼ full with water. Add fat until it reaches the 1 cup mark and drain off the water.

Quantities of seasoning often cannot be specified exactly and should therefore be judged according to taste.

Index

Page references to photographs are printed in **heavy** type. All soups are listed only under SOUP(S).

Note: all quantities given are for 4 servings unless otherwise stated.
Approximate metric equivalents to all measures are given in brackets.

Rice

Paella

Ingredients: *1 quart (1 l) mussels · 3½ tablespoons oil · a 2-lb (1-kg) chicken · 4 oz (115 g) veal · 4 oz (115 g) beef · 2 onions, chopped · 1½ lb (750 g) prawns · 2 green peppers, deseeded and quartered · salt · pepper · 1–2 zucchini, peeled and diced · 6 oz (175 g) tomatoes, peeled and diced · 3 oz (90 g) sausage, peeled and sliced · 2 cloves of garlic, peeled and crushed · ½ lb (225 g) rice · 2 teaspoons saffron · ½ lb (225 g) peas · 4 artichoke hearts, sliced · few olives, pitted*

Wash and scrub the mussels thoroughly and cook in a little oil over high heat until the shells have opened. Drain and shell, reserving a few in their shells for garnish. Strain the cooking liquid through a fine cloth and reserve. Cut the chicken into 8 pieces and cube the meats. Sauté the meat in a frying pan, preferably an iron one, in remaining hot oil (step 1). Add the onions, raw prawns, green peppers, salt and pepper (step 2). Mix well and cook the mixture, covered, for 10 minutes. Add the zucchini, tomatoes, sausage, garlic and the reserved cooking liquid from the mussels. Cover pan and cook over low heat for 1 hour and 10 minutes. Add the rice and saffron (step 3) and boiling water to cover. Cook covered, over low heat for 10 minutes. Add the peas, artichoke hearts, shelled mussels and a few olives, and continue cooking for 10 minutes. Add reserved mussels. Serves 6–8.

Rice à la Grècque

Heat 2 oz (60 g) butter in a flameproof earthenware casserole with a cover. Add 1 onion, chopped finely, and cook without browning. Add 1 clove of garlic, peeled and crushed, 4 lettuce leaves, shredded, 2 tablespoons dried mushrooms, softened in lukewarm water, squeezed dry and sliced, 2–3 tomatoes, peeled and chopped, 4 oz (115 g) sausage, peeled and chopped, or sausage meat, ¾ lb (350 g) rice, 2 pints (1 l) hot stock, salt and pepper. Cover the casserole and bake in a hot oven (400°F/gas 6) for 20–25 minutes. When cooked, add 1 tablespoon melted butter, 6 oz (175 g) cooked peas, 1 diced red pepper and 3 tablespoons raisins, cooked in a little butter.

2

3

Risotto Novara

Ingredients: *$\frac{3}{4}$ lb (350 g) rice • 6 oz (175 g) dried red or kidney beans, soaked in cold water for 12 hours • $\frac{3}{4}$ lb (350 g) cabbage • 2 celery sticks • 1 carrot • 3 tomatoes • 2 oz (60 g) bacon rind, scalded and chopped • 4 pints (2 l) water • 1 stock cube, if desired • salt • 1 salami, or sausage • 2 oz (60 g) bacon • 1 slice onion • 1 oz (30 g) butter • $\frac{1}{2}$ glass red wine • pepper*

Clean the cabbage and cut into pieces, slice the celery and carrot, chop the tomatoes (step 1), and put all the vegetables in a large pan with the drained beans, bacon rind, water, stock cube, if using, and salt. Cover pan and cook over low heat for about 2 hours. Chop the salami or sausage, bacon, and onion (step 2), and sauté in the butter in another pan. Add the rice and cook the mixture for a few minutes. Add the wine and let evaporate. Continue cooking the rice, adding the vegetables and stock gradually as required, stirring occasionally (step 3), until rice is *al dente.* Add pepper to taste. Transfer to a warm serving dish, let stand for a few minutes and serve.

Rice Valencienne

Sauté 3 oz (90 g) onion, finely chopped, in 1 oz (30 g) butter until golden. Add 2 cloves of garlic, peeled and crushed, and a generous pinch saffron. Add 6 oz (175 g) rice, stirring with a wooden spatula. Add 1 pint ($\frac{1}{2}$ l) chicken stock or water and 6 oz (175 g) peas. Bring to the boil, cover and bake in a moderate oven (350°F/gas 4) for 15–18 minutes. Separate the rice grains with a fork and gently mix in 1 oz (30 g) butter. Transfer to a warm serving dish and serve immediately.

Rice with Sausage and Celery

Sauté $\frac{1}{2}$ onion, chopped, in 1 oz (30 g) butter. Add 4 oz (115 g) sausage, peeled and chopped, or sausage meat, and 6 oz (175 g) celery sticks, finely chopped. Cook for a few minutes. Add 2 teaspoons tomato sauce, thinned with a little hot water, and cook the mixture over low heat for about 40 minutes. Add $\frac{3}{4}$ lb (350 g) rice and continue cooking, adding 3 pints ($1\frac{1}{2}$ l) stock gradually, as required, stirring occasionally, until the rice is *al dente.* Blend in 1 oz (30 g) butter and a few tablespoons grated Parmesan cheese. Transfer to a warm serving dish and serve immediately.

1

2

3

1

2

3

Risotto Chartreuse

Ingredients: for the risotto, *¾ lb (350 g) rice • 1 lb (500 g) prawns • 1 leek, 1 sliced onion, 1 celery stick, 1 small carrot and parsley, all chopped together • 1 clove of garlic, peeled and quartered • 2 oz (60 g) butter • 2 tablespoons oil • salt • pepper • 3 pints (1½ l) fish stock*

For the fish: *4–6 perch fillets • flour • 1 slice onion • 2 oz (60 g) butter • ½ glass dry white wine • 8 oz (225 g) canned peeled tomatoes, coarsely chopped • salt • pepper*

Cook the prawns in boiling salted water until tender. Drain, reserving the cooking liquid. Shell and devein, reserving 8–10 in their shells for decoration, and cut in small pieces (step 1). Pound the shells in a mortar (step 2), return to reserved liquid and cook for 10–15 minutes. Strain and reserve liquid. Sauté the vegetables and garlic in 1½ oz (45 g) butter and the oil. Add the reserved liquid, salt and pepper and cook gently for 10 minutes. Discard garlic. Add the rice, cook for a few minutes and add the prawns, reserving about 2 oz (60 g). Pour in the fish stock gradually, stirring occasionally, and cook until rice is *al dente*.

Sauté the onion in the butter, and discard. Lightly flour the fish fillets, add to pan and sauté lightly without drying. Add the wine, and let evaporate. Add the tomatoes, reserved prawns, salt and pepper. Cover pan and cook mixture for about 15 minutes. Remove rice from heat, add remaining butter and pile rice onto a warm serving dish. Place the fish fillets around the risotto, garnish with reserved prawns and pour tomato sauce over (step 3).

Rice alla Pilota

Cook 2 sausages, peeled and chopped, or about ½ lb (225 g) sausage meat, chopped, in 2 oz (60 g) butter over low heat for about 1 hour. Bring a deep pan of lightly salted water to the boil, and using a sheet of paper rolled into a cone, pour in ¾ lb (350 g) rice slowly so that the rice forms a cone in the middle of the pan. With a ladle remove water until water remaining just covers the point of the cone. Bring mixture to the boil, cook for a few minutes and remove pan from heat. Add the sausage mixture, 1½ tablespoons grated Parmesan cheese, a pinch of cinnamon and mix gently. Cover the rice with a folded cloth and cover pan. Wrap pan in a towel and let stand for 20–25 minutes. Add salt if necessary and serve immediately.

Risotto with Shellfish

Ingredients: *$\frac{3}{4}$ lb (350 g) rice · 1 pint ($\frac{1}{2}$ l) mussels · 1 lb (500 g) clams · 6 oz (175 g) prawns · 1 tablespoon oil · celery, carrot and onion, all chopped together · 3 oz (90 g) butter · 1 small glass brandy · $\frac{1}{2}$ pint ($\frac{1}{4}$ l) dry white wine · salt · pepper · 1 slice onion, chopped · $2\frac{1}{2}$ pints ($1\frac{1}{4}$ l) stock*

Wash and scrub the mussels and clams thoroughly. Cook in the oil over high heat until the shells have opened (step 1), drain, reserving the cooking liquid, and shell. Shell and devein the prawns. Sauté the chopped vegetables in 2 oz (60 g) butter and the brandy, add the wine and let reduce by half. Add the prawns, mussels, clams (step 2), salt, pepper and a little of the reserved cooking liquid from the mussels and clams, strained through a sieve. Cook mixture over a moderate heat for 15 minutes, stirring occasionally.

In another pan, sauté the slice onion in the remaining butter, add the rice, and the stock gradually as required, and cook, stirring occasionally, until the rice has absorbed the cooking liquid. Place the rice on a warm serving dish and pour the shellfish sauce over (step 3), arranging shellfish attractively. Serve immediately.

Risotto with Prawns

Shell and devein $\frac{3}{4}$ lb (350 g) prawns, reserving shells. Sauté 1 celery stalk, 1 onion, 1 carrot, all chopped, and 1 clove of garlic, peeled, in 2 oz (60 g) butter for a few minutes. Discard the garlic. Add $\frac{1}{2}$ pint ($\frac{1}{4}$ l) dry white wine and the reserved shells, bring mixture to the boil and cook over low heat for 10 minutes. Add $3\frac{1}{2}$ pints ($1\frac{3}{4}$ l) boiling salted water, cover, and continue cooking for about 30 minutes. In another pan sauté 1 slice chopped onion in 2 oz (60 g) butter for a few minutes, add the prawns, and cook for 3–4 minutes. Add $\frac{3}{4}$ lb (350 g) rice, cook for a few minutes, then add the shell stock, strained through a sieve, gradually as required. Cook, stirring occasionally, until the rice is *al dente*. Transfer to a warm serving dish, and serve with grated Parmesan cheese in a separate dish.

1 

2 

3 

Risotto Milanese

Ingredients: *¾ lb (350 g) rice · 2 oz (60 g) beef marrow · 1 slice onion, chopped · 3 oz (90 g) butter · ½ glass dry white or red wine (optional) · saffron to taste · 3 pints (1½ l) hot stock · a few tablespoons grated Parmesan cheese*

Sauté the beef marrow and onion in half the butter over moderate heat (step 1), add the wine, if using, and let reduce by half. Add the rice, cook for a few minutes, add the saffron and stock gradually as required (step 2), stirring occasionally. Cook the rice over high heat until it is *al dente*, then blend in the remaining butter and the Parmesan cheese (step 3). Transfer risotto to a warm serving dish and let stand for a few minutes before serving.

Rice with Sage

Cook ¾ lb (350 g) rice in 3 pints (1½ l) boiling salted water until it is *al dente*. In a pan sauté 2 cloves of garlic, peeled and crushed, and a few leaves fresh sage in 3 oz (90 g) butter for a few minutes. Place the rice in a warm deep serving dish; sprinkle with grated Parmesan cheese. Stir in garlic and sage mixture, mix gently and serve.

Risotto Parmigiana

Sauté 1 slice onion, chopped, in 2 oz (60 g) butter, add ¾ lb (350 g) rice and cook for a few minutes. Add 3 pints (1½ l) boiling meat stock gradually as required and continue cooking the rice, stirring occasionally, until it is *al dente*. Remove the risotto from the heat, and blend in 1 oz (30 g) butter and a generous amount of grated Parmesan cheese.

Rice with Tomatoes and Mussels

Scald ½ lb (225 g) tomatoes in boiling water, peel, and drain and chop. Wash and scrub 2 lb (1 kg) mussels thoroughly and cook them in 1 pint (½ l) water, 3 oz (90 g) onion, chopped, and salt and pepper over moderate heat until the shells have opened. Remove the mussels from the pan and discard the shells. Add 1 clove of garlic, chopped, the chopped tomatoes and 6 oz (175 g) rice to the pan and cook over low heat for 18–20 minutes without stirring. Add mussels, mix and serve.

1

2

3

1

2

3

Pilaff

Ingredients: *10 oz (300 g) rice · 3 tablespoons onion, finely chopped · 4 oz (115 g) butter · 1½ pints (¾ l) hot stock*

In an ovenproof casserole cook the onion in half the butter without browning. Add the rice and stir until transparent (step 1). Add the stock and bring the mixture to the boil. Cover the casserole (step 2), and bake in a hot oven (400°F/gas 6) for 15–20 minutes without stirring. Remove the rice from the oven, transfer to a warm serving dish, add the remaining butter and separate the grains with a fork (step 3). Serve immediately.

Pilaff with Sweetbreads

Wash 10 oz (300 g) sweetbreads thoroughly and cook in boiling salted water for 10 minutes. Drain, cool and remove and discard tubes and membranes. Slice, flour the slices lightly and sauté in 2 oz (60 g) butter until golden on both sides. Sprinkle with Marsala and allow to evaporate. Add a little stock and cook over low heat for 20 minutes. Prepare a pilaff following the basic recipe above, place on a warm serving dish in a dome. Pour the sweetbreads and their sauce on top and sprinkle with finely chopped parsley. Serve immediately.

Rice à la Turque

Sauté 3 oz (90 g) salt pork, diced, and 1 onion, finely chopped, for a few minutes. Add 1 clove of garlic and 2 tomatoes, both peeled and chopped, and continue cooking the mixture for a few minutes. Add about 3 oz (90 g) chicken livers, quartered, cook for a few minutes, remove and reserve. Stir in 1 tablespoon flour, salt and cayenne pepper and pour in 12 fl oz (300 ml) white wine. Add a pinch of thyme and 1 bay leaf, crushed, and cook the mixture over low heat for 30 minutes. Strain the mixture through a sieve, return to the heat and add 6 oz (175 g) rice. Cook the rice for 15–18 minutes until it is *al dente*. Add reserved chicken livers, mix gently, transfer to a warm serving dish, sprinkle with chopped parsley, if liked, and serve immediately.

2

3

Risotto with Peas

Ingredients: *¾ lb (350 g) rice · 2 lb (1 kg) fresh peas or ¾ lb (350 g) canned or frozen peas · 2 oz (60 g) bacon, diced · 1 slice onion and 1 sprig parsley, both chopped · 2 oz (60 g) butter · 2 tablespoons oil · 3 pints (1½ l) hot stock · grated Parmesan cheese · salt · pepper*

Shell the peas (step 1), if using fresh peas. Sauté the bacon, onion and parsley in half the butter and the oil for a few minutes (step 2), add the peas and cook the mixture for 1 minute. Add the rice (step 3), and cook until transparent. Add the stock gradually as required, and continue cooking the rice, stirring occasionally, until it is *al dente*. Blend in the remaining butter and Parmesan cheese, sprinkle with salt and pepper, transfer to a warm serving dish and serve immediately.

Risotto with Mushrooms

Sauté 1 slice onion, chopped, in 2 oz (60 g) butter for a few minutes, add ¾ lb (350 g) fresh mushrooms, wiped, trimmed and sliced (or 3 tablespoons dried mushrooms, softened in lukewarm water for 30 minutes, squeezed dry and sliced), and cook the mixture for a few minutes. Add ¾ lb (350 g) rice and ½ glass dry white wine and let evaporate. Add 3 pints (1½ l) hot stock gradually as required and continue cooking the mixture, stirring occasionally, until the rice is *al dente*. Remove the risotto from the heat, stir in 1 oz (30 g) butter and grated Parmesan cheese, transfer the mixture to a warm serving dish and allow to stand for 1 minute. Sprinkle with grated Parmesan cheese, and serve immediately.

Risotto with Spinach

Clean, wash and cook 10 oz (300 g) spinach in boiling salted water until tender, and drain. Sauté ½ clove of garlic, peeled, and parsley, both chopped, in 1 oz (30 g) butter for a few minutes, add the spinach and ¾ lb (350 g) rice, mixing well. Add 3 pints (1½ l) hot stock gradually as required, and continue cooking, stirring occasionally, for about 15 minutes or until the rice is *al dente*. Blend in 1 oz (30 g) butter and a generous amount grated Parmesan cheese, transfer to a warm serving dish and serve immediately.

Risotto with Asparagus Tips

Ingredients: *¾ lb (350 g) rice · 2 lb (1 kg) asparagus · 3 oz (90 g) butter · 3 pints (1½ l) hot stock · 1 slice onion, chopped · parsley, chopped · grated Parmesan cheese*

Scrape and wash the asparagus, halve them, and reserve the tips (step 1). Cut half remaining asparagus sticks into small pieces. In a pan melt 2 oz (60 g) butter, add the asparagus pieces and cook for a few minutes. Add the rice (step 2), continue cooking, stirring occasionally, and adding a little stock as required, until rice is *al dente*. In another pan melt 1 oz (30 g) butter, add the chopped onion and cook for a few minutes. Add the asparagus tips and cook, adding a little stock occasionally, until asparagus is tender. Sprinkle with chopped parsley. Remove risotto from heat, stir in remaining butter and some grated Parmesan cheese and transfer to a warm serving dish, arranging in a dome shape. Place the asparagus tips vertically around the risotto (step 3), and serve immediately.

Genoese Risotto

Sauté ½ onion, chopped, in 2 oz (60 g) butter until golden, add 6 oz (175 g) fresh sausage, peeled and sliced, or sausage meat, ½ lb (225 g) fresh peas and the tender part of 1 artichoke, finely sliced. Cook for a few minutes. Add 2 tablespoons dried mushrooms, softened in lukewarm water, squeezed dry and sliced, 4 oz (115 g) canned peeled tomatoes, a little hot stock, salt and pepper. Bring the mixture to the boil, covered, and cook for about 20 minutes. Boil ¾ lb (350 g) rice in salted water for 8 minutes, drain and add to the sauce. Blend in 2 tablespoons grated Parmesan cheese and 1½ pints (¾ l) hot stock and pour the mixture into an oiled mould or casserole. Bake in a hot oven (400°F/gas 6) for 15 minutes. Sprinkle with blended breadcrumbs and Parmesan cheese, and return to oven to gratiné.

Rice Pompadour

In a flameproof casserole sauté 2 small onions, chopped, in 1 oz (30 g) butter, add 1 clove of garlic, peeled and crushed, 3 oz (90 g) mushrooms, finely sliced, and cook for a few minutes. Add 6 oz (175 g) rice, salt, pepper and 1 pint (½ l) hot water, cover and bring to the boil. Bake in a hot oven (400°F/gas 6) for 15 minutes. Stir in 6 oz (175 g) chicken meat, diced, 4 fl oz (100 ml) double cream and ½ oz (15 g) butter. Garnish with olives.

1

2

3

Country Timbale

Ingredients: for the sauce, *2 tablespoons dried mushrooms softened in lukewarm water, squeezed dry and sliced • 1 clove of garlic, peeled • 1 oz (30 g) butter • 1 small glass brandy • stock*

For the meatballs: *6 oz (175 g) minced beef • 2 oz (60 g) chopped ham • 1 handful white bread, soaked in milk and squeezed dry • 1 egg yolk • 2 tablespoons grated Parmesan cheese • salt • grated nutmeg • flour • butter*

For the risotto: *¾ lb (350 g) rice • 1 slice onion, chopped • 2 oz (60 g) butter • 3 pints (1½ l) hot stock • 2 eggs • grated Parmesan cheese, to taste • breadcrumbs • 6 oz (175 g) fresh ricotta cheese, sliced • melted butter*

Sauté the mushrooms and the garlic in the butter for a few minutes. Discard the garlic, sprinkle mushrooms with brandy and let it evaporate. Add a little stock and continue cooking until sauce has thickened.

Prepare the meatballs: in a bowl mix the minced beef with the ham, bread, egg yolk, Parmesan cheese, salt and grated nutmeg. Using the fingers, make walnut-sized balls, flour lightly and cook in butter until evenly golden.

Prepare the risotto: sauté the onion in the butter for a few minutes, add the rice and cook until transparent. Add ⅔ of the stock and cook the rice, stirring occasionally, adding the remaining stock gradually as required until rice is *al dente*. Remove from the heat, blend in the eggs, 4 tablespoons Parmesan cheese (steps 1 and 2), and spread rice out on an oiled baking sheet to cool without further cooking.

Butter a high-sided mould and dust it lightly with breadcrumbs. Line the bottom and sides with risotto, reserving a little. Fill the mould with alternate layers of meatballs, mushroom sauce, ricotta cheese (step 3), Parmesan cheese to taste and butter curls. Cover with the reserved risotto, sprinkle with breadcrumbs and add a little melted butter. Bake the timbale in a hot oven (400°F/gas 6) for about ½ hour. Unmould on a warm serving dish.

1

2

3

1

2

3

Pasta

Ravioli

Ingredients: for the pasta, *1 lb (500 g) sifted flour • 4 eggs • 6 tablespoons water*

For the filling: *10 oz (300 g) beef • 1 oz (30 g) bacon • 2½ oz (75 g) pork fillet • 2 oz (60 g) butter or margarine • onion, celery, carrot, all chopped together • salt • pepper • ½ glass dry white wine • ½ lb (225 g) Savoy cabbage • 2½ oz (75 g) mortadella • 1 handful white bread soaked in milk and squeezed dry • milk • 1 egg • grated Parmesan cheese • grated nutmeg*

For the sauce: *meat sauce or gravy from a roast or braised meat • grated Parmesan cheese for sprinkling*

For the filling: 1 day before serving, put the beef, barded with the bacon, in a pan with the pork, butter or margarine, onion, celery and carrot, and sauté over moderate heat, turning the meat occasionally, until all the ingredients are golden. Add salt and pepper to taste and the white wine, and cook the mixture, covered, over very low heat for 2 hours. Remove the meat from the pan and reserve. Add the cabbage, cooked in boiling salted water for 10 minutes, to the pan and sauté for a few minutes. Work the cabbage, meats and mortadella through the medium blade of a food chopper. Add the white bread, egg, grated Parmesan cheese, salt, pepper and grated nutmeg to taste, and blend well.

Make a dough of the flour, eggs and water (see p.39), and roll out thinly. Shape the filling into small balls and set them about 2 inches apart on the dough (step 1). Fold the dough over (step 2) and cut with a ravioli or biscuit cutter (step 3) or with a small glass. Seal the edges. Cook the ravioli in boiling salted water until it is *al dente*, drain, and put on a dish. Cover with meat sauce or gravy and sprinkle with Parmesan. Serves 5–6.

Genoese Ravioli

Boil 4 oz (115 g) each of endives and spinach in salted water for 5 minutes and drain. Dice 6 oz (175 g) veal, 2½ oz (75 g) pork, 3 oz (90 g) sweetbreads, scalded and peeled, and sauté in 2 oz (60 g) butter for a few minutes. Add a piece of brain, scalded and peeled, and 1 oz (30 g) beef marrow and cook for a few minutes. Chop with marjoram and pound in a mortar. Add 2 oz (60 g) sausage meat, a little bread, soaked in milk and squeezed, grated Parmesan cheese and salt, and mix. Prepare dough and proceed as above.

Macaroni with Mushrooms

Ingredients: *$\frac{3}{4}$ lb (350 g) macaroni · $\frac{1}{2}$ lb (225 g) fresh mushrooms or 2 tablespoons dried mushrooms, softened in lukewarm water, drained and sliced · 2 oz (60 g) butter · $\frac{1}{2}$ glass brandy · stock · 3–4 triangles processed cheese cut in pieces · 3 tablespoons grated Parmesan cheese · 1 glass milk · salt · pepper ·*

Clean, trim and finely slice the fresh mushrooms, if using (step 1). Sauté mushrooms in $\frac{1}{2}$ oz (15 g) butter for a few minutes, add the brandy (step 2) and let it evaporate. Add $1\frac{1}{2}$ tablespoons stock and cook the mixture over low heat for 25 minutes. Cook the macaroni in boiling salted water until it is *al dente*. Heat the remaining butter in a large pan, add the processed cheese, Parmesan cheese and milk (step 3), and cook the mixture until it is creamy. Add the mushroom mixture, salt and pepper to taste and continue cooking the mixture, stirring constantly, until it is well blended. Add the drained macaroni, mix gently and transfer to a warm serving dish. Serve immediately.

Macaroni Marinara

Slice 4 oz (115 g) green olives, pitted, in thin strips. In a pan heat 3 oz (90 g) butter, add 1 clove of garlic, peeled, and sauté for a few minutes. Discard garlic. Add 2 anchovy fillets, desalted, and parsley, chopped, and cook the mixture over low heat for a few minutes. Add the olives and 10 oz (300 g) canned peeled tomatoes and cook the sauce for about 10 minutes. Cook $\frac{3}{4}$ lb (350 g) macaroni in boiling salted water until it is *al dente*, drain and add to sauce. Sprinkle with freshly ground pepper, transfer to a serving dish and serve.

Macaroni with Meatballs

Mix 6 oz (175 g) minced beef with 1 handful white bread, soaked in milk and squeezed dry, 1 egg yolk, 2 tablespoons grated Parmesan cheese, salt and grated nutmeg. Using the fingers, make walnut-sized balls, roll in flour and cook in boiling oil until evenly golden on all sides. In a saucepan heat 1 oz (30 g) butter with 1 tablespoon olive oil, add a little onion, chopped, $\frac{3}{4}$ lb (350 g) canned peeled tomatoes, salt and pepper to taste. Cook the sauce for about 20 minutes, add the meatballs and continue cooking the mixture for a few minutes. Cook $\frac{3}{4}$ lb (350 g) macaroni in boiling salted water until it is *al dente*, drain thoroughly and mix the macaroni gently with the sauce. Sprinkle with grated Parmesan cheese, if liked, transfer to a warm serving dish and serve immediately.

2

3

1

2

3

Gratinéed Cannelloni

Ingredients: for the dough, *1 lb (500 g) sifted flour · 4 eggs · 3 tablespoons water*

For the filling: *2 oz (60 g) butter · 1 slice onion, chopped · 2 oz (60 g) ham, chopped · ¾ lb (350 g) beef, diced · ½ bay leaf · 1 tablespoon flour · stock · salt · pepper · grated nutmeg · 1 egg · 1 handful white bread, soaked in milk and squeezed dry · Parmesan cheese · tomato or béchamel sauce · butter · grated Parmesan cheese*

Prepare the dough (see p.39) and let stand. Roll out thinly and cut into 4 or more 5-inch by 4-inch rectangles. Cook these, a few at a time, in boiling salted water until tender, drain (step 1), and place on a damp cloth. In a pan heat the butter, add the onion and ham and cook for a few minutes. Add the beef and the bay leaf and cook for a further few minutes. Stir in the flour, add a little stock, salt, pepper and grated nutmeg to taste. Cook the mixture over low heat for 45 minutes, discard the bay leaf. Work mixture through the medium blade of a food chopper, add the egg, the bread and grated Parmesan cheese and work mixture until well blended. Put a little filling on each rectangle and roll up (step 2). Place the cannelloni side by side in a buttered ovenproof dish. Cover with tomato sauce (step 3) or with a rather thin béchamel sauce, dot with butter and sprinkle with grated Parmesan cheese. Gratiné the cannelloni in a hot oven (400°F/gas 6) until golden. Serve immediately.

Cannelloni Maison

Prepare 12 little crêpes: in a bowl mix 2 eggs with 4½ oz (130 g) sifted flour and 1 pinch salt, add ½ pint (¼ l) milk or water and 1 tablespoon melted butter gradually. Beat the batter with a wire whisk until smooth. Heat a 7-inch frying pan and add a little oil. Pour in 2 tablespoons batter and quickly tilt and rotate the pan so that the batter coats the bottom thinly and evenly. Cook the crêpe on both sides until golden. Continue until all the batter is used. Prepare a béchamel sauce with 2 oz (60 g) butter or margarine, 2 oz (60 g) sifted flour, 1 pint (½ l) milk, salt, pepper and grated nutmeg to taste. Remove from heat and stir in 2½ tablespoons grated Gruyère cheese. Pour a little béchamel sauce onto each crêpe, add ½ slice ham to each and roll up crêpes. Place side by side in a buttered ovenproof dish, add 8 fl oz (200 ml) double cream and sprinkle with grated Parmesan cheese. Bake in a hot oven (400°F/gas 6) for 15 minutes and serve immediately.

2 

3 

Pasta Shells with Cream Cheese and Ham

Ingredients: *$\frac{3}{4}$ lb (350 g) pasta shells · 2 oz (60 g) butter at room temperature · 4 oz (115 g) ricotta cheese · 4 oz (115 g) cream cheese · 2 oz (60 g) ham or tongue · salt*

In a bowl beat the butter, add the cheeses and salt to taste and beat the mixture until it is light and foamy (step 1). Cut the ham or tongue into thin strips (step 2) and add it to the cheese mixture. Cook the pasta shells in boiling salted water until they are *al dente*, drain and mix gently in a warm serving dish with the cheese mixture (step 3). Serve very hot.

Shells with Basil

In a small pan cook 2 oz (60 g) butter, 1 stock cube and a few tablespoons water over moderate heat for a few minutes. Add 3 triangles processed cheese and continue cooking the mixture, stirring constantly, until the cheeses have melted. Stir in 1 generous tablespoon fresh basil, chopped, and pour the sauce onto $\frac{3}{4}$ lb (350 g) pasta shells, cooked in boiling salted water until they are *al dente* and drained. Serve immediately on a warm serving dish.

Stuffed Shells

Cook 10 oz (300 g) giant pasta shells in boiling salted water with 1 tablespoon oil until they are *al dente* and drain on a cloth. Prepare a béchamel sauce with 2 oz (60 g) butter, 2 oz (60 g) sifted flour, 1 pint ($\frac{1}{2}$ l) milk, salt and grated nutmeg to taste. Add 4 oz (115 g) fontina or Gruyère cheese, diced, and cook the sauce until the cheese is melted. Blend in 2 egg yolks and fill the shells with the mixture. Place the shells, filled side up, in a buttered oven-proof dish. Add a little melted butter, sprinkle with grated Parmesan cheese and bake in a hot oven (400°F/gas 6) for 20 minutes or until golden. Serve immediately.

Shells Niçoise

Scald 3 tomatoes in boiling water, drain and peel. Halve them and drain again. In a pan heat 3 tablespoons oil, add 1 onion, chopped, 1 clove of garlic, peeled and crushed, the tomatoes, $\frac{1}{2}$ pint ($\frac{1}{4}$ l) water, a pinch of thyme and basil, chopped and 1 bay leaf. Cook over moderate heat for 20 minutes. Cook $\frac{1}{2}$ lb (225 g) pasta shells in boiling salted water until they are *al dente*; drain. Stir in 2 oz (60 g) butter and cover with the sauce. Transfer to a warm serving dish and sprinkle with a little grated Gruyère cheese.

Gratinéed Macaroni

Ingredients: *¾ lb (350 g) short macaroni · ½ onion · 3 oz (90 g) butter · 6 oz (175 g) minced beef · 2 bay leaves · ½ lb (225 g) canned peeled tomatoes · salt · pepper · stock · 2 tablespoons grated Parmesan cheese*

For the béchamel sauce: *1 oz (30 g) butter · 1 tablespoon flour · ½ pint (¼ l) milk · salt · grated nutmeg · 1 egg, beaten · 2 tablespoons grated Parmesan cheese*

Chop the onion (step 1) and sauté in butter until golden. Add the beef and bay leaves (step 2) and cook for a few minutes. Add the tomatoes, salt and pepper to taste, and cook for about 1 hour, adding a little stock occasionally. Remove the sauce from heat and add the grated Parmesan cheese. Cook the macaroni in boiling salted water until it is *al dente*, drain and blend with the sauce. Pour into a buttered ovenproof dish. Make a béchamel sauce with the butter, flour, milk, salt and grated nutmeg, remove from the heat, stir in the beaten egg and the grated Parmesan cheese. Pour over the macaroni (step 3) and bake in a moderate oven (350°F/gas 4) for 40–45 minutes or until top is golden and crisp. Serve immediately.

Baked Macaroni with Cauliflower

Sauté 1 small onion, chopped, in 2 oz (60 g) butter until golden, add 6 oz (175 g) minced beef and cook for a few minutes. Add a few tablespoons tomato sauce, thinned with a little water, salt and pepper to taste, and cook for about 15 minutes. Cut 1 cauliflower into small flowerets and parboil in boiling salted water. Remove and reserve flowerets. Add ¾ lb (350 g) short macaroni to the cooking water and cook until *al dente*. Drain and mix gently with ½ the sauce and 2 tablespoons grated Parmesan cheese. Sauté the flowerets in 3 oz (90 g) butter until golden. Butter an ovenproof dish, dust with breadcrumbs and fill with alternate layers of macaroni, cauliflower, sauce, and grated Parmesan cheese to taste. Bake in a hot oven (400°F/gas 6) for 15 minutes or until top is golden and crisp. Serve immediately in the cooking dish.

1

2

3

Orecchiette with Turnip Leaves

Ingredients: *¾ lb (350 g) sifted flour · 6 oz (175 g) semolina · salt · lukewarm water · ¾ lb (350 g) turnip leaves · olive oil · black pepper*

Work the flour and semolina with enough salted lukewarm water to make a fairly solid dough, like bread dough. Cover to prevent drying. Using a little dough at a time, form rolls 1 inch in diameter and 15 inches in length (step 1). Slice the rolls (step 2) and, using the round edge of a knife, pull out one edge of each slice on the board, forming little ears (*orecchiette*) by shaping the slices with the thumb. Cook the orecchiette in boiling salted water, add the turnip leaves and continue cooking until the orecchiette are *al dente*. Drain the mixture (step 3) and add olive oil and freshly ground black pepper to taste. Transfer to a warm serving dish and serve immediately.

Orecchiette with Meat Sauce

Pound 4 slices stewing beef for a few minutes. Put a few strips of bacon and pecorino or Parmesan cheese on each slice. Sprinkle with garlic and parsley, chopped. Roll up the slices and tie them with heavy thread. In a frying pan heat a little oil, add a little onion, chopped, and sauté for a few minutes. Add the beef rolls and sauté until evenly golden. Add ½ glass red or dry white wine and let it evaporate. Add a little stock and ¾ lb (350 g) canned peeled tomatoes, worked through a sieve, and continue cooking the rolls over low heat until the sauce has thickened. Cook ¾ lb (350 g) orecchiette in boiling salted water until they are *al dente*, drain and mix gently with the meat sauce. Transfer to a warm serving dish and serve immediately. Serve the rolls separately.

Apulian Orecchiette

Cook 2 lb (1 kg) fresh tomatoes, peeled, seeded and drained, ½ onion, sliced, 2 cloves of garlic, peeled and crushed, a few basil leaves and salt to taste, covered, for 30 minutes. In another pan sauté a little onion, sliced, 2 cloves of garlic and 2 bay leaves in 4 tablespoons oil for a few minutes. Discard the bay leaves. Add 1¼ lb (600 g) beef or veal in one piece and cook until evenly golden. Add ½ glass red wine and the tomato mixture, worked through a sieve, and cook, covered, over low heat for 1½ hours, adding a little stock if necessary. Remove the meat, cut 1 slice, chop and add to the sauce. Cook ¾ lb (350 g) orecchiette in boiling salted water until they are *al dente*, drain and mix gently with the meat sauce and a little grated pecorino cheese. Transfer to a warm serving dish and serve immediately. Serve the meat separately.

1

2

3

1

2

3

'Straw-and-Hay' with Cream and Ham

Ingredients: *6 oz (175 g) each of green and white pasta ('straw-and-hay') · 3 oz (90 g) butter · 8 fl oz (100 ml) cream · 4 tablespoons grated Parmesan cheese · salt · grated nutmeg · 3 oz (90 g) ham, diced*

Straw-and-hay consists of equal measures of pasta prepared with spinach (green) and pasta prepared with egg (white). It resembles thin noodles (step 1). Cook the pasta in boiling salted water until it is *al dente*. In a large pan cook the butter, cream, Parmesan cheese, salt, grated nutmeg to taste and diced ham over moderate heat, stirring constantly, until the mixture has the consistency of a thick cream (step 2). Drain the pasta, add to the pan and mix gently but thoroughly (step 3). Transfer to a warm serving dish, and serve immediately.

Gratinéed Straw-and-Hay

Cook $\frac{3}{4}$ lb (350 g) straw-and-hay, if fresh, or 10 oz (300 g) if dried, in boiling salted water until it is *al dente*; drain. Sauté 1 slice onion, chopped, in 1 oz (30 g) butter and 1 tablespoon oil until transparent. Add 3 oz (90 g) ham, diced, salt and pepper to taste and cook for a few minutes. Add 6 oz (175 g) canned peeled tomatoes, worked through a sieve, and cook for a further 15 minutes. In a separate pan, cook 4 oz (115 g) peas in boiling salted water until they are tender and add them to the sauce. Butter an ovenproof casserole, put a layer of pasta in the bottom, add half the sauce and cover with a few slices of Emmenthal cheese. Add the remaining pasta, the remaining sauce, a few more slices of Emmenthal cheese and dot with butter curls. Bake in a hot oven (400°F/gas 6) for 15 minutes or until the top is golden. Serve immediately.

Straw-and-Hay Nests

Cook 10 oz (300 g) straw-and-hay in boiling salted water until it is *al dente*, drain and transfer to a deep dish. Mix in 1 tablespoon grated Parmesan cheese, 2 oz (60 g) ham, chopped, and 3 eggs, beaten with salt and pepper. Pour on a buttered dish and let it cool. Divide the pasta into 12 equal parts and twirl each part on a fork to form a nest. Sprinkle the nests with flour and flatten them slightly with the palm of the hand. Pick up the nests with a slotted spatula and sauté them in 4 oz (115 g) butter until golden on both sides. Serve immediately with a tomato sauce in a sauceboat.

Baked Lasagne

Ingredients: for the pasta, *1 lb (500 g) sifted flour · 4 eggs · 1 lb (500 g) spinach*

For the sauce: *4 oz (115 g) butter or margarine · 1 carrot, 1 celery stick, 1 onion, all chopped together · 6 oz (175 g) minced beef · salt · pepper · grated nutmeg · ½ pint (¼ l) milk · tomato sauce*

For the béchamel sauce: *2 oz (60 g) butter or margarine · 2 tablespoons flour · 1 pint (½ l) milk · salt · grated nutmeg · Parmesan*

Heat half the butter or margarine, add the onion, celery and carrot, and cook until golden. Add the beef, salt, pepper and nutmeg to taste and cook the mixture for 20 minutes. Add the tomato sauce, thinned with a little hot water, cover the pan and simmer until the tomato sauce is well blended. Add the milk and cook, covered, over low heat for 1 hour.

Meanwhile prepare the dough (see p.39) with the flour, eggs and spinach, cooked in boiling salted water, drained well and worked through a sieve. Roll out the dough in a very thin sheet and cut into 3½-inch squares (step 1). Make the béchamel sauce with the butter or margarine, flour, milk, salt and grated nutmeg to taste, remove from the heat and stir in 2–3 tablespoons grated Parmesan cheese. Cook the lasagne, a few at a time, in boiling salted water with 1 oz (30 g) butter or margarine so that the squares do not stick, for a few minutes (step 2), wash under cold running water, drain and dry on a clean cloth. Grease a baking dish with butter or margarine, add a layer of lasagne, cover with a little béchamel sauce, a little meat sauce (step 3), grated Parmesan cheese and curls of butter or margarine. Continue until all the ingredients are used. Bake in a hot oven (400°F/gas 6) until top is golden. Serves 5–6.

Lasagne 16th Century Style

Prepare and cook the dough as above using ¾ lb (350 g) sifted flour and 3 eggs.

Wash and pat dry ¾ lb (350 g) perch or sole fillets, dip them in egg beaten with salt, then in breadcrumbs and sauté them lightly. Prepare a béchamel sauce with 2 oz (60 g) butter, 2 tablespoons flour, 1 pint (½ l) milk, salt and grated nutmeg, remove from heat and stir in 2 tablespoons grated Gruyère cheese. Grease a baking dish, add a layer of lasagne, cover with béchamel sauce and add a few fish fillets. Continue in this manner until all the ingredients are used. Add curls of butter and bake in a moderate oven (350°F/gas 4) for about 30 minutes or until the top is golden.

2

3

Macaroni and Pigeon Pie

Ingredients: *10 oz (300 g) macaroni · 2 oz (60 g) butter · grated Parmesan cheese · 12 oz (350 g) shortcrust pastry, home-made or frozen*

For the sauce: *1 oz (30 g) butter · 1 slice onion, chopped · 1 tablespoon dried mushrooms soaked in lukewarm water, squeezed dry and sliced · 2 pigeons or other small birds, cleaned and cut in pieces · 2 oz (60 g) Italian prosciutto, chopped · salt · pepper · 1 small glass Marsala or dry white wine · stock*

For the béchamel sauce: *1 oz (30 g) butter · 2 tablespoons flour · ½ pint (¼ l) milk · salt · pepper · grated nutmeg*

Prepare the sauce by heating the butter in a pan, add the onion, mushrooms, pigeon pieces, prosciutto, salt and pepper to taste, and sauté the mixture until all ingredients are golden. Add the Marsala or white wine and let evaporate. Add a little stock and cook gently, covered, for 35–40 minutes.

Meanwhile, cut the macaroni into 4-inch pieces, cook in boiling salted water until *al dente* and drain. When the pigeon sauce is cooked, remove the pigeon pieces, bone and reserve. Mix the sauce gently with the macaroni, 2 oz (60 g) butter and grated Parmesan cheese. Divide the dough into 2 pieces, one slightly larger than the other, and roll each out thinly. Butter a 12-inch pie pan and line with the smaller piece of dough (step 1). Add ⅔ of the macaroni mixture, the reserved pigeon pieces (step 2), cover with the remaining macaroni and add the béchamel sauce. Sprinkle with Parmesan cheese and cover with the second piece of dough, pressing edges together. Cut shapes from any remaining dough to decorate top of pie. Brush with the beaten egg (step 3), prick surface with a fork and bake in a moderate oven (350°F/gas 4) for 1 hour, or until golden. Let stand for 3–4 minutes before unmoulding on a warm dish. Serve grated Parmesan cheese separately. Serves 6.

1

2

3

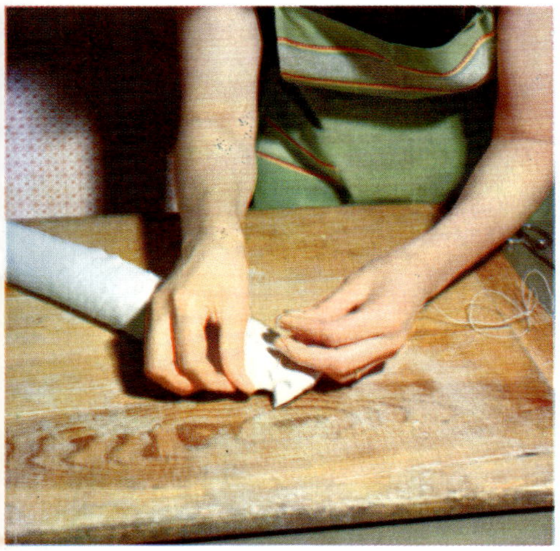

Spinach Roll

Ingredients: for the pasta,
¾ lb (350 g) sifted flour · 2 eggs ·
4 tablespoons lukewarm water · salt

For the filling: *1 lb (500 g) spinach · salt ·*
6 oz (175 g) ricotta cheese ·
6 oz (175 g) grated Parmesan cheese · 2 eggs ·
grated nutmeg

To finish: *tomato sauce ·*
grated Parmesan cheese or 4 oz (115 g) butter, clarified

Sift the flour on a board, make a well in the centre and add the eggs, water and salt. Work ingredients together until well blended, form the dough into a ball, wrap in wax paper and let stand for about ½ hour.

Meanwhile, prepare the filling: clean and wash the spinach and cook without water, with a little salt. Drain thoroughly and work through a sieve with the ricotta cheese. In a bowl blend this mixture with the Parmesan cheese, eggs, salt and grated nutmeg to taste. Roll out the dough in a thin rectangle, cover with the spinach mixture (step 1) and roll up (step 2). Roll in a clean cloth (step 3) and tie both ends with string (step 4). Cook in simmering salted water for about 1 hour, transfer to a warm serving dish and serve, sliced, with tomato sauce and grated Parmesan cheese or clarified butter poured over the spinach roll.

Cheese Strudel

Sift 10 oz (300 g) flour on a board, make a well in the centre and add 1 egg and 5 tablespoons water. Blend ingredients thoroughly, form the dough into a ball, wrap in wax paper and let stand for ½ hour. Meanwhile, in a bowl beat 3 eggs for a few minutes, add 3 oz (90 g) soft butter, 6 tablespoons breadcrumbs, ½ pint (¼ l) milk, salt and grated nutmeg to taste, and blend well. Roll out the dough thinly on a floured cloth, cover with the egg mixture and sprinkle evenly with 4 tablespoons grated Parmesan cheese. Lifting one edge of the cloth, roll up the strudel, sealing the edges with a little milk or water, and roll it round into the form of a snail. Tie the four corners of the cloth together and cook the strudel in boiling salted water for 45 minutes. Remove the cloth, cut the strudel in quarters and serve with 4 tablespoons clarified butter and grated Parmesan cheese to taste.

Spaghetti with Shellfish

Ingredients: *¾ lb (350 g) spaghetti · 1 lb (500 g) mussels · 2 oz (60 g) butter · 10 oz (300 g) prawns · 2 cloves of garlic, peeled · 1 tablespoon dried mushrooms, soaked in lukewarm water, squeezed dry and sliced · 2 tablespoons tomato paste · 3 oz (90 g) tuna fish in olive oil · salt · pepper · chopped parsley*

Wash and scrub the mussels (step 1) and cook them, covered, over high heat with 1 oz (30 g) butter until all the shells have opened. Drain, reserving the liquid, and shell. Strain the cooking liquid through a fine sieve, bring to the boil, add the prawns and cook for about 5 minutes. Drain the prawns, reserving the liquid, shell and devein them and add them to the cooked mussels. In another pan, sauté the cloves of garlic in the remaining butter for a few minutes and discard. Add the mushrooms and cook for a few minutes. Add the tomato paste and the mussel and prawn cooking liquid, gradually, and cook the sauce over low heat until it has thickened. Add the tuna fish, reserved mussels and prawns, salt to taste and a generous amount of freshly ground pepper (step 2). Cook the sauce until all the ingredients are heated through. Cook the spaghetti in boiling salted water until it is *al dente*, drain, mix with the sauce (step 3) and mix in some chopped parsley. Transfer to a warm serving dish, sprinkle with the remaining parsley, and serve immediately.

Spaghetti with Oil and Garlic

In a small pan cook 4 tablespoons oil, 1–2 cloves of garlic, peeled and crushed, and a generous amount freshly ground pepper over very low heat. Remove pan from heat as soon as the garlic starts to brown and pour the sauce on ¾ lb (350 g) spaghetti, cooked in boiling salted water until it is *al dente* and drained. Add a generous amount of chopped parsley and serve immediately.

Spaghetti with Clams

Wash and scrub 2 lb (1 kg) clams thoroughly. Cook them in 1 tablespoon oil, covered, over high heat until all the shells have opened, without allowing oil to boil. Drain, reserving the liquid, and discard shells. Sauté 1 clove of garlic, peeled, in 3 oz (90 g) butter for a few minutes, add a generous amount chopped parsley, 8 oz (225 g) canned peeled tomatoes, worked through a sieve, and pepper to taste, and cook the mixture for about 5 minutes. Add the reserved liquid and continue cooking the sauce until it has thickened. Remove and discard the garlic, add the clams and cook the sauce for 1 minute. Pour the sauce on ¾ lb (350 g) spaghetti, cooked in boiling salted water until it is *al dente* and drained. Transfer to a warm serving dish, and serve immediately.

1

2

3

2

3

Spaghetti with Artichoke Sauce

Ingredients: *¾ lb (350 g) spaghetti • 2–3 artichokes • juice of 1 lemon • 1 slice onion, chopped • 4 tablespoons oil • ¾ lb (350 g) canned peeled tomatoes • salt • pepper •*

To garnish: *chopped parsley*

Wash the artichokes, discard the hard outer leaves and trim the spiky ends. Halve them, discard the chokes, slice horizontally (step 1), and soak the slices in water with lemon juice to prevent discoloration. Sauté the onion in the oil for a few minutes, add the drained artichokes and cook the mixture over low heat for a few minutes. Add the tomatoes, drained and chopped, salt and pepper to taste and cook the sauce over low heat (step 2) for 35–40 minutes. Pour the sauce on the spaghetti, cooked in boiling salted water until it is *al dente* and drained, sprinkle with parsley (step 3) and serve immediately.

Macaroni with Ricotta Cheese

Cook ¾ lb (350 g) macaroni in boiling salted water until it is *al dente*. In a deep serving dish mix 5 oz (150 g) ricotta cheese with ½ teaspoon cinnamon and 1 oz (30 g) butter and thin the mixture with a few tablespoons cooking water from the pasta. Drain the macaroni add to cheese mixture, season with salt and pepper to taste, and serve.

Macaroni with Gravy

Cook ¾ lb (350 g) macaroni in boiling salted water until it is just *al dente*; drain. Place a layer of macaroni in a buttered baking dish, cover with gravy from a roast, sprinkle with grated Parmesan cheese and continue in this manner until all ingredients are used up. Add butter and bake in a hot oven (400°F/gas 6) until golden on top.

Spaghetti Printanière

Cook ¾ lb (350 g) spaghetti in boiling salted water until it is *al dente*; drain. Chop ½ lb (225 g) tomatoes coarsely and slice 1 fresh mozzarella cheese thinly. Pour the mixture on the spaghetti, add a generous amount of fresh basil leaves, salt and freshly ground pepper, and serve.

Macaroni with Zucchini Sauce

In 2 oz (60 g) butter cook ¾ lb (350 g) small zucchini, sliced, over low heat without letting them brown. Remove the zucchini from the heat and mix in 2 eggs, beaten with 2 tablespoons milk, 4 tablespoons grated Parmesan cheese, salt and pepper. Mix the sauce with ¾ lb (350 g) macaroni, cooked in boiling salted water until it is *al dente* and drained. Serve immediately.

Spaghetti with Eggplant

Ingredients: *¾ lb (350 g) spaghetti · 1 clove of garlic, peeled · 1 slice onion · oil · 1 oz (30 g) butter · 1 lb (500 g) canned peeled tomatoes · salt · pepper · a few basil leaves · 4 eggplants · grated Parmesan cheese*

To garnish: *sprig of fresh basil (optional)*

Sauté the garlic and onion in oil and the butter, discard garlic and add the tomatoes (step 1). Add salt and pepper to taste and cook over low heat for 1½ hours. Add basil leaves. Slice the eggplants and fry quickly in boiling oil (step 2). Pour the tomato sauce on the spaghetti, cooked in boiling salted water until it is *al dente* and drained, sprinkle with grated Parmesan cheese and garnish with the eggplant slices (step 3). Mix well, top with sprig of fresh basil, if liked. Serve immediately.

Spaghetti alla Romana

Sauté 1–2 cloves of garlic, peeled and thinly sliced, and 1 piece of hot pepper in 2 oz (60 g) butter for a few minutes, add 2 anchovies, desalted and mashed, and let soften. Add ¾ lb (350 g) fresh tomatoes, peeled, seeded and coarsely chopped, 1 tablespoon capers, washed under cold running water, and 4 oz (115 g) pitted black olives. Cook the sauce over low heat for 8–10 minutes and pour on ¾ lb (350 g) spaghetti, cooked in boiling salted water until it is *al dente* and drained.

Spaghetti with Peas

Sauté 1 onion, thinly sliced, in 3 oz (90 g) butter for a few minutes, add 8 oz (225 g) canned peeled tomatoes and cook the mixture for 10 minutes. Add a few lettuce leaves, chopped, and cook for a further 15 minutes. Add 4 oz (115 g) canned peas, salt and pepper to taste and cook for 8–10 minutes. Mix the sauce with ¾ lb (350 g) spaghetti, cooked in boiling salted water until *al dente* and drained.

Three-Flavoured Spaghetti

Sauté 1 tablespoon dried mushrooms, soaked in lukewarm water, squeezed dry and sliced, or 6 oz (175 g) fresh mushrooms, thinly sliced, in 2 oz (60 g) butter for a few minutes. Add 2 oz (60 g) ham, cut into thin strips, 4 oz (115 g) fresh peas and a little stock, and cook the sauce over low heat for ½ hour. Mix the sauce with ¾ lb (350 g) spaghetti, cooked in boiling, salted water until it is *al dente* and drained, and serve with grated Parmesan cheese.

1

2

3

Noodles Bolognese

Ingredients: for the pasta, *1 lb (500 g) sifted flour · 4 eggs · 5 oz (150 g) spinach, cooked and chopped (optional)*

For the sauce: *2 oz (60 g) bacon, chopped · 2 oz (60 g) butter · 1 celery stick, 1 carrot and ½ onion, all chopped together · 6 oz (175 g) minced beef · a few dried mushrooms, soaked in lukewarm water, squeezed dry and sliced (optional) · ½ glass white or red wine · salt · pepper · grated nutmeg · 2 tablespoons tomato paste · stock or water · 1 glass milk (optional)*

Prepare the pasta: sift the flour on a lightly floured board, make a well in the centre and break in the eggs (step 1). Add the spinach if green noodles are required. Work flour and eggs together with a round-bladed knife (step 2) until a smooth dough is formed. Roll out, not too finely (step 3). Let dough dry for a few minutes then fold over to form a 4-inch wide strip and cut into ¼-inch strips. Pick up 5–6 strips at one time, shake out gently and let dry on the board (step 4).

Prepare the sauce: in a pan sauté the bacon in the butter for a few minutes, add the chopped vegetables and cook until they start to brown. Add the beef and mushrooms (if using), and cook for a few minutes. Stir in the wine, add salt, pepper and nutmeg to taste, and cook the sauce until wine has evaporated. Add the tomato paste, thinned with some stock or water, and cook, covered, over very low heat for about 2 hours, adding a little more stock or water occasionally. Add the milk (if using) gradually and continue cooking for 1 hour. Pour the sauce on the noodles, cooked in boiling salted water until they are *al dente* and drained. Mix well and serve immediately.

Curried Noodles

Sauté 1 medium onion, finely chopped, in 3 oz (90 g) butter without browning. Add 2 teaspoons curry powder, salt, and 3 oz (90 g) ham, chopped, and cook the mixture for a few minutes. Pour the seasonings on ¾ lb (350 g) noodles, cooked in boiling salted water until *al dente* and drained. Mix well and serve immediately. Serve grated Parmesan cheese separately.

Green Noodles with Cheese

Ingredients: *$\frac{3}{4}$ lb (350 g) green noodles · 2 oz (60 g) Emmenthal · 2 oz (60 g) Gouda or other Dutch cheese · 2 oz (60 g) Parmesan · 2 oz (60 g) mozzarella · 3 oz (90 g) butter, melted · salt · pepper · grated Parmesan*

Dice all the cheeses (step 1), and melt the butter. Cook the pasta in boiling salted water until it is *al dente*, drain and put on a warm serving dish. Stir in the diced cheese (step 2), pepper to taste and half the butter. Mix quickly (step 3), add the remaining butter, sprinkle with grated Parmesan and serve immediately.

Baked Noodles with Artichokes

In a saucepan cook 1 oz (30 g) butter with 1$\frac{1}{2}$ tablespoons flour and stir in $\frac{1}{2}$ pint ($\frac{1}{4}$ l) stock until the mixture is smooth. Add 1 onion, stuck with 1 clove, 1 celery stick and 1 small carrot, both sliced, 1 bay leaf, pepper to taste and a pinch of thyme. Simmer the mixture slowly for 25–30 minutes. In a large pan heat 1 oz (30 g) butter and add 8–10 artichoke hearts, cut into thin strips, in one layer only. Add salt and pepper to taste and cook the artichokes over low heat, adding a little stock if necessary. Remove the sauce from the heat and, using a wooden spoon, stir in 4 fl oz (100 ml) cream. Strain through a sieve into another pan and stir in 2 egg yolks, one at a time, and 4 triangles of processed cheese, melted in 2 tablespoons milk. Put $\frac{3}{4}$ lb (350 g) green noodles in boiling salted water, return to the boil and drain. Pour pasta in a bowl and mix in 1 oz (30 g) butter and $\frac{3}{4}$ of the white sauce. Arrange 3 layers of pasta and 2 layers of cooked artichokes in a buttered baking dish. Pour in the remaining white sauce, sprinkle with grated Parmesan cheese and bake in a hot oven (400°F/gas 6) until the top is golden.

Golden Noodles

Cook $\frac{3}{4}$ lb (350 g) noodles in boiling salted water until they are *al dente*; drain. In a bowl beat 3 eggs with 1 glass milk, 3$\frac{1}{2}$ tablespoons grated Parmesan cheese and 3 oz (90 g) butter, melted. Add 3 triangles of processed cheese, diced, 3 oz (90 g) ham, diced, salt and pepper and the pasta. Transfer to a buttered baking dish, sprinkle with grated Parmesan cheese and add butter curls. Bake in a hot oven (400°F/gas 6) for 25 minutes.

1

2

3

Creamy Tortellini

Ingredients: for the pasta, *1 lb (500 g) sifted flour · 4 eggs · 2 tablespoons water*

For the filling: *3 oz (90 g) pork, chopped · 2 oz (60 g) turkey or chicken breast, chopped · 2 oz (60 g) butter · 3 oz (90 g) Italian prosciutto · 3 oz (90 g) mortadella · 2 oz (60 g) beef marrow · 1 egg · salt · grated nutmeg*

For the sauce: *3 oz (90 g) butter · 8 fl oz (200 ml) cream · 6 tablespoons grated Parmesan cheese · salt · grated nutmeg*

Prepare the dough: sift the flour on a board, make a well in the centre, break in the eggs and add the water. Work ingredients together until smooth, cover and let stand.

Meanwhile, prepare the filling: cook the pork and turkey or chicken meat in the butter, chop finely together with the prosciutto, mortadella and beef marrow, and work mixture through a sieve. Blend in the egg and salt, and nutmeg to taste. Roll out dough into a thin sheet and cut into 2½-inch squares (step 1). Put a little filling in the centre of each square and fold squares over so as to form triangles, pressing edges firmly together. Twist each triangle around one finger, pressing the 2 lower corners firmly one on top of the other (step 2). Gather dough trimmings together, roll out into a thin sheet and repeat process until all dough and filling is used up. Cook the tortellini in boiling salted water until *al dente*.

Prepare the sauce: in a large pan heat the butter, cream, Parmesan cheese and salt and grated nutmeg to taste, over a moderate heat, stirring constantly. Drain the pasta, add to the pan (step 3) and cook until sauce has thickened. Serve immediately on a warm dish.

Tortelloni Parma Style

Halve a 3-lb (1½-kg) pumpkin and discard the seeds. Cook in the oven until tender, and peel. In a bowl mash the pulp with 3 oz (90 g) crushed macaroons, 4 oz (115 g) grated Parmesan cheese, 1 or 2 eggs, the grated peel of ½ lemon, and salt to taste.

Prepare a dough as for above recipe, using 1 lb (500 g) sifted flour, 2 eggs, and 6 tablespoons water. Roll out dough into a thin sheet and put walnut-sized mounds of the filling on half the dough. Fold dough over and pat it down so that no air is trapped. Cut filled dough in rectangles, pressing the edges together and pressing the 2 opposite corners one on top of the other. Cook in boiling salted water and drain. Toss in melted butter and grated Parmesan cheese and serve immediately.

2

3

1

2

3

Thin Tortelloni with Cheese

Ingredients: for the pasta, *1 lb (500 g) sifted flour · 3 eggs · 8 tablespoons water*

For the filling: *¾ lb (350 g) ricotta or other white cheese, sieved · 6 tablespoons grated Parmesan cheese · 2 eggs · parsley, chopped · salt · grated nutmeg*

To finish: *4 oz (115 g) butter, melted · 4 tablespoons grated Parmesan cheese*

Prepare the filling: in a bowl mix the cheeses, eggs, parsley and salt and nutmeg to taste.

Prepare the pasta: sift the flour on a board, make a well in centre, break in the eggs and add the water. Work ingredients together until dough is smooth, roll out into a thin sheet and cut into circles with a pasta or biscuit cutter (step 1). Put a little filling on each circle (step 2), fold over, pressing the edges together, and press the corners together to form tortelloni (step 3). Cook the tortelloni in boiling salted water for a few minutes and remove them with a slotted spoon as they rise to the surface. Toss in the melted butter and Parmesan cheese and serve immediately. Serves 5–6.

Tortellini with Cream and Mushrooms

In a bowl blend 6 oz (175 g) ricotta cheese, 2½ oz (75 g) capon breast or pork, finely chopped and cooked in butter, 3 tablespoons grated Parmesan cheese, 1 egg plus 1 egg yolk, a little grated lemon rind, salt, pepper and grated nutmeg. Prepare the dough with 12 oz (350 g) flour, 3 eggs and water as above. Roll out thinly and cut in 3-inch squares. Put a little filling on each square and fold over to form triangles. Twist each triangle around one finger, pressing lower corners firmly together.

Cook 2 oz (60 g) dried mushrooms, soaked in lukewarm water and squeezed dry, in 1 oz (30 g) butter for a few minutes. Sprinkle with ½ glass brandy and flame. Add some stock and cook gently for 25 minutes.

Cook the tortellini in boiling salted water until *al dente*. In a large pan heat 2 oz (60 g) butter, add 8 fl oz (200 ml) cream, 6 tablespoons grated Parmesan cheese, salt and grated nutmeg to taste and the mushroom mixture, and cook for a few minutes, stirring constantly. Drain pasta, add to pan, heat through and serve.

2

3

Vol-au-vent with Tortellini

Ingredients: *a 10-inch round vol-au-vent • 1 lb (500 g) fresh tortellini • 1 slice onion • 2 oz (60 g) butter • 8 oz (225 g) canned peeled tomatoes, worked through a sieve • stock • 4 fl oz (100 ml) cream • 3½ tablespoons grated Parmesan cheese • grated nutmeg*

Sauté the onion in ½ the butter and discard. Add tomatoes and some stock and cook for ½ hour. Boil the tortellini in salted water and drain. In a casserole heat remaining butter, add the tomato sauce, cream, Parmesan cheese, nutmeg and tortellini (steps 1 and 2). Reheat gently. Heat the vol-au-vent in a hot oven (400°F/gas 6) for a few minutes, fill with the tortellini (step 3), add the pastry cover and serve immediately.

Tortellini Timbale

Prepare a dough with ¾ lb (350 g) sifted flour, 5 oz (150 g) butter, 1 egg, 6 tablespoons milk and salt, and let stand.

Cook 3 oz (90 g) beef or veal marrow in boiling water for 3 minutes, drain and dice. Melt 1 oz (30 g) butter, add 2 tablespoons dried mushrooms softened in lukewarm water, squeezed dry and coarsely chopped, the marrow and 2 tablespoons Marsala and cook the mixture for a few minutes. Add 4 fl oz (100 ml) stock and continue cooking over low heat for 25 minutes, adding a little more stock if necessary.

Prepare a béchamel sauce with 2 oz (60 g) butter, 2 oz (60 g) flour, 3 fl oz (75 ml) milk, salt and grated nutmeg to taste. Parboil 1 lb (500 g) tortellini in boiling salted water, drain and toss in 1 oz (30 g) butter, 8 fl oz (200 ml) cream and grated Parmesan cheese. Roll out ⅔ of prepared dough into a 20-inch circle and use to line a 12-inch pie pan, buttered and sprinkled with breadcrumbs. Add ½ the tortellini, ½ the marrow sauce mixed with the béchamel sauce, and sprinkle with grated Parmesan cheese. Repeat the procedure with remaining ingredients and cover with remaining dough, rolled out into a circle. Press edges together firmly and prick the surface with a fork. Brush with egg yolk and bake in a hot oven (400°F/gas 6) for 25–40 minutes. Let stand for a few minutes before unmoulding.

Gnocchi à la Parisienne

Ingredients: for the pasta, *1 pint (½ l) milk* • *3½ oz (100 g) butter* • *salt* • *grated nutmeg* • *10 oz (300 g) sifted flour* • *5–6 eggs* • *5½ tablespoons grated Parmesan cheese*

For the mornay sauce: *2 oz (60 g) butter* • *2 tablespoons flour* • *1 pint (½ l) milk* • *salt* • *grated nutmeg* • *1 egg yolk* • *3 slices Emmenthal cheese, chopped, or 5 tablespoons grated Gruyère cheese*

To finish: *1 oz (30 g) butter, melted* • *4 tablespoons grated Parmesan cheese*

Prepare the pasta: in a large pan bring the milk, butter and salt and grated nutmeg to taste to the boil, pour the sifted flour in all at once and cook mixture, stirring constantly, until it leaves the sides of the pan (step 1). Remove pan from heat and let cool slightly. Add the eggs, one at a time, and the Parmesan cheese, beating vigorously; allow to cool.

Prepare the mornay sauce with the butter, flour, milk and salt and grated nutmeg to taste, and remove from heat. Stir in the egg yolk, cheese and remaining butter. Using a pastry bag fitted with a large round tube, pipe the dough out, cutting it off in 1-inch lengths with a knife dipped in hot water (step 2), to fall into a large pan of boiling salted water. Remove the gnocchi with a slotted spoon as they rise to the surface, and drain. Pour a thin layer of mornay sauce into an ovenproof dish, add the gnocchi, cover with remaining sauce (step 3), and sprinkle with melted butter and grated Parmesan cheese. Cook in a hot oven (400°F/gas 6) for 15 minutes or until golden.

Gnocchi Roll

Work 1 lb (500 g) boiled potatoes through a potato ricer. Blend in 1 egg, 6 oz (175 g) sifted flour and a little salt and work mixture until smooth. Place dough on a lightly floured cloth and roll it out ½ inch thick. Cover the dough with 6 oz (175 g) fontina or Bel Paese cheese, sliced; roll up, wrap in the cloth and tie securely at both ends. Cook in boiling salted water for 25 minutes. Serve in slices with melted butter and grated Parmesan cheese, or with tomato sauce.

Spinach Gnocchi

Wash and cook 1½ lb (750 g) fresh spinach without water. Drain and work through a food chopper into a bowl. Add 10 oz (300 g) ricotta or other white cheese, 2 eggs plus 2 egg yolks, 6 oz (175 g) sifted flour, a generous handful of grated Parmesan cheese and salt and grated nutmeg. Stir well. Shape mixture into small balls and sprinkle with flour. Drop into boiling salted water and remove with a slotted spoon as they rise to the surface. Put on individual plates and sprinkle with grated Parmesan cheese to taste. Heat 3 oz (90 g) butter with 1 clove of garlic, peeled, cook until golden, discard garlic and pour sauce over gnocchi.

1

2

3

Potato Gnocchi

Ingredients: for the gnocchi, *2 lb (1 kg) potatoes* · *12 oz (350 g) flour* · *1 egg* · *salt*

For the sauce: *1 oz (30 g) butter* · *1 tablespoon oil* · *1 slice onion, chopped* · *6 oz (175 g) pork sausage, peeled and chopped, or sausage meat* · *1 bay leaf* · *$\frac{3}{4}$ lb (350 g) canned peeled tomatoes, worked through a sieve* · *salt* · *pepper* · *stock* · *grated Parmesan cheese*

Cook the potatoes in boiling salted water until tender, peel and work through a potato ricer (step 1). Add the flour, egg, and salt to taste, and work mixture until well blended. Shape into finger-sized cylinders, cut into thick slices (step 2) and press against a cheese grater (step 3). Sprinkle with flour, drop into boiling water and remove as they rise to the surface.

Prepare the sauce: cook the butter, oil and onion for a few minutes, add the sausage or sausage meat and cook for a few minutes. Add the bay leaf, tomatoes and salt and pepper to taste, and cook for $\frac{1}{2}$ hour, adding a little stock if necessary. Discard bay leaf, pour sauce over gnocchi on a serving dish and sprinkle with grated Parmesan cheese

Sicilian Gnocchi

Slice 10 oz (300 g) stale bread and let soak in 1 pint ($\frac{1}{2}$ l) hot milk for about $1\frac{1}{2}$ hours. Drain, squeeze dry if necessary, and mash with a fork. In a bowl beat 2 eggs, add the bread, 3 oz (90 g) Italian prosciutto or smoked bacon, diced, 2 tablespoons grated Parmesan cheese, 3 tablespoons flour, and salt and a little chopped parsley to taste, and stir mixture until well blended. With fingers dipped in water, shape mixture into small eggs. Sift 6 oz (175 g) flour on a board and roll the gnocchi in the flour until well coated. Drop into boiling salted water and remove with a slotted spoon as they rise to the surface. Transfer to a warm serving dish and serve immediately tossed in melted butter and grated Parmesan cheese.

Potato Gnocchi with Cheese

Prepare the gnocchi as for the basic recipe above and cook in boiling salted water. Drain. Dice 6 oz (175 g) fontina, Bel Paese or Gruyère cheese. Put the gnocchi on individual plates, add a generous handful of diced cheese and sprinkle with grated Parmesan cheese. Heat 2 oz (60 g) butter with 1 clove of garlic, peeled, until golden; discard garlic and pour butter over gnocchi. Serve very hot.

2

3

1

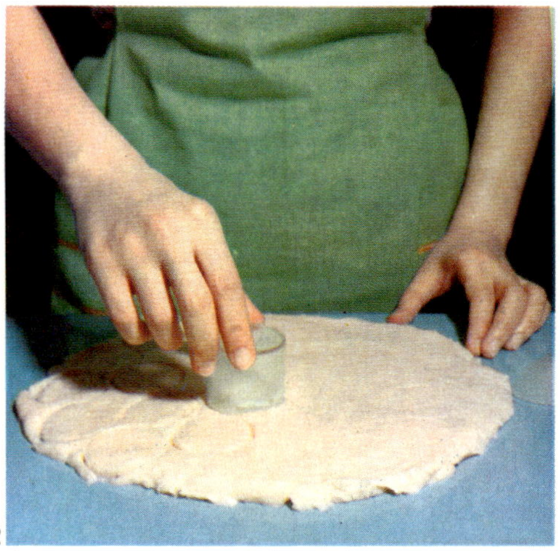

2

3

Gnocchi alla Romana

Ingredients: for the pasta, *3 oz (90 g) butter* · *salt* · *grated nutmeg* · *½ lb (225 g) semolina* · *2 tablespoons grated Parmesan cheese* · *2–3 egg yolks, mixed with a little milk*

To finish: *2 oz (60 g) butter, melted* · *6 tablespoons grated Parmesan cheese*

Bring the milk, butter, and salt and grated nutmeg to taste, to the boil, and gradually pour in the semolina (step 1), stirring constantly. Cook over moderate heat for 15–20 minutes, stirring constantly. Remove pan from heat and stir in the Parmesan cheese and egg yolks. Pour mixture onto a marble slab or baking sheet sprinkled with water, flatten to the thickness of a finger with a spatula dipped in water and let cool. Using a small biscuit cutter or glass, cut mixture into circles (step 2), place circles in layers (step 3) in a buttered ovenproof dish, covering each layer with melted butter and Parmesan cheese. Bake in a hot oven (400°F/gas 6) for about ½ hour or until golden on top.

Quick Gnocchi

Bring ½ pint (¼ l) water and 1 teaspoon salt to the boil, add ½ pint (¼ l) milk and pour the liquid into a bowl containing 1 envelope potato flakes. Let stand for 1 minute and blend until smooth. Add 1 tablespoon flour, 2 eggs, lightly beaten, 5 tablespoons grated Parmesan cheese and a little grated nutmeg, and work the mixture until smooth. With wet fingers, form into egg shapes and flatten them. Butter an ovenproof dish, sprinkle the bottom and sides with breadcrumbs, place a layer of gnocchi in the bottom, cover with 1 oz (30 g) butter, melted, and sprinkle with grated Parmesan cheese. Add another layer of gnocchi, melted butter and Parmesan cheese, and bake in a hot oven (400°F/gas 6) for ½ hour.

Gnocchi with Prunes

Prepare potato gnocchi as for the basic recipe above. Soak dried prunes in lukewarm water until tender, pit them and fill with a little sugar. Shape the potato dough into fairly large balls, putting a prepared prune in the middle of each. Cook the gnocchi in boiling salted water as above, and drain. Toss in breadcrumbs sautéed in butter, sugar and cinnamon.

Polenta

Plain Polenta

Ingredients: *$3\frac{1}{2}$ quarts ($3\frac{1}{2}$ l) water, or $\frac{1}{2}$ water, $\frac{1}{2}$ milk • 1 handful of rock salt • 2 lb (1 kg) maize meal*

Bring the water and salt to the boil in a pan. Gradually pour in the maize meal (step 1), stirring constantly and always in the same direction (step 2) until the mixture binds together. Turn the polenta out onto a wooden board or block (step 3) and slice with a string or a wooden knife.

Polenta can also be poured into variously shaped moulds and then unmoulded.

If little time is available, polenta can also be made in a pressure cooker. Serves 8.

Polenta is very good served with jugged hare or rabbit.

Polenta with Cheese

Prepare the polenta following the basic recipe above, with 1 small handful of rock salt and $1\frac{1}{2}$ lb (750 g) maize meal. Cook for 45–50 minutes, stirring constantly. Stir in 10 oz (300 g) fontina or Gruyère cheese and 4 oz (115 g) butter, both diced, and cook for 5–10 minutes, or until well blended. Transfer to a warm serving dish and cover with 3 oz (90 g) butter, melted. Serve immediately. Serves 6–8.

Polenta with Mushrooms

In a small pan sauté 1 clove of garlic in 1 oz (30 g) butter until golden, discard garlic and add 2 tablespoons dried mushrooms soaked in lukewarm water, squeezed dry and sliced, or $\frac{1}{2}$ lb (225 g) fresh mushrooms, coarsely chopped or sliced. Cook for about 20 minutes, adding a little stock if necessary.

Prepare a béchamel sauce, using 2 oz (60 g) butter, 2 tablespoons flour, 1 pint ($\frac{1}{2}$ l) milk, and grated nutmeg to taste. Remove from heat and add 2 tablespoons grated Parmesan cheese, and salt and pepper to taste. Mix $\frac{3}{4}$ of the sauce with the mushrooms and blend well. Butter an ovenproof dish and fill with alternate layers of thin slices of mozzarella and grated Parmesan cheese, about 1 lb (500 g) thinly sliced cold polenta and the mushroom béchamel. Finish with a layer of plain béchamel sauce, a few tablespoons grated Parmesan cheese and butter curls. Bake in a moderate oven (350°F/gas 4) for 45 minutes.

Polenta with Gorgonzola

Sauté $\frac{1}{2}$ onion in butter; add 6 oz (175 g) Gorgonzola cheese, crumbled, and a little milk. Cook until cheese is melted. In an ovenproof dish, layer polenta and cheese sauce. Bake in a hot oven (400°F/gas 6) for 35 minutes.

2

3

Grandmother's Polenta

Ingredients: for the polenta, *3½ pints (1¾ l) water · rock salt · 1 lb (500 g) maize meal · 3 oz (90 g) butter*

For the stuffing: *1 lb (500 g) sweetbreads, skinned and diced · flour · 1 slice onion, chopped · 3 oz (90 g) butter · ½ glass Marsala · stock · 1 lb (500 g) fresh mushrooms, sliced, or 2 tablespoons dried mushrooms, soaked in lukewarm water, squeezed dry and sliced · salt · pepper*

To finish: *4 oz (115 g) Italian prosciutto, thinly sliced · 1 egg, beaten · 3½ tablespoons grated Parmesan cheese · butter curls*

Prepare the polenta (see p.47): bring the water to the boil in a large pan, gradually pour in the maize meal, stirring constantly, and cook the mixture over high heat for about 45–50 minutes, stirring constantly with a wooden spoon to prevent lumps forming. Add the butter during last minutes of cooking and pour the polenta into a buttered high-sided mould. Leave to cool.

Meanwhile, prepare the filling: sprinkle the sweetbreads with flour and sauté them with the onion in almost all the butter for a few minutes (step 1). Add the Marsala, let it reduce, add a little stock and cook for about 20 minutes. Add the mushrooms and a little more stock and cook until thick. Season with salt and pepper to taste.

Unmould the polenta and turn it upside down, and with a knife make a circular incision around the middle, leaving a 1-inch border.

Slice the middle part thinly, without cutting all the way through to the bottom, and remove slices carefully (step 2), leaving a polenta shell. Brush the mould with remaining butter and line with prosciutto slices; brush with the beaten egg. Return polenta shell to mould and fill with layers of sweetbread sauce, polenta slices, grated Parmesan cheese (step 3) and butter curls. Finish with polenta slices and prosciutto slices. Bake in a hot oven (400°F/ gas 6) for 35–40 minutes and unmould onto a warm serving dish. Serves 4–6.

1

2

3

2

3

Vegetable Moulds and Soufflés

Spinach and Carrot Mould

Ingredients: for the spinach mould, *1 lb (500 g) spinach · 1 egg · 1 oz (30 g) butter · 1 tablespoon flour · 3 fl oz (75 ml) milk · salt · grated nutmeg ·* $\frac{1}{2}$ *teaspoon potato starch · 1 tablespoon grated Parmesan cheese*

For the carrot mould: $\frac{1}{2}$ *lb (225 g) carrots · 1 oz (30 g) butter · 1 tablespoon flour · 3 fl oz (75 ml) milk · 1 tablespoon grated Parmesan cheese · salt · grated nutmeg · 2 eggs*

Cook the spinach in boiling salted water for a few minutes, work through a sieve (step 1), leave to cool, then mix in the egg yolk, reserving the white. Make a béchamel sauce with the butter, flour, milk and salt and grated nutmeg to taste, and blend into the spinach, together with the potato starch and Parmesan cheese.

Cook the carrots in boiling salted water until tender, work through a sieve (step 2), then sauté in butter for a few minutes. Add the flour, stirring constantly, then the milk a little at a time off the heat. Cook over low heat for 10 minutes. Remove from heat, stir in the Parmesan cheese, and salt and grated nutmeg to taste, and leave to cool. Add 2 egg yolks, reserving the whites, and beat the mixture for 10 minutes.

Add 2 egg whites, beaten until stiff, to carrot mixture and 1 egg white, also beaten until stiff, to spinach mixture. Butter a high-sided ovenproof mould and carefully pour in the spinach mixture and the carrot mixture, without mixing them (step 3). Bake in a bain-marie in a moderate oven (350°F/gas 4) for about 1 hour. Unmould and serve immediately.

Other vegetables, such as cauliflower, may also be used in this manner to make vegetable moulds.

Cheese Soufflé

Ingredients: *3 oz (90 g) butter • 3 oz (90 g) flour • 1 pint ($\frac{1}{2}$ l) boiling milk • 2 tablespoons grated Parmesan cheese • 3 oz (90 g) grated Gruyère cheese • salt • 4 eggs*

Heat the butter in a pan, add the flour and cook for a few minutes. Add the milk and cook, stirring constantly, for 5 minutes. Remove from heat, add cheeses and salt (step 1). Beat the egg yolks until foamy and add gradually. Beat the egg whites until stiff, then fold in gently (step 2). Pour into a soufflé dish, buttered and lightly sprinkled with flour (step 3) and bake in a hot oven (400°F/gas 6) for 20 minutes or until risen and golden on top. Serve immediately.

Asparagus Soufflé

Cook the tender parts of 1 lb (500 g) asparagus in boiling salted water for a few minutes, drain and place in a buttered soufflé dish. Heat $\frac{1}{2}$ pint ($\frac{1}{4}$ l) milk with 3 slices onion and $\frac{1}{2}$ bay leaf; strain. In a pan heat $2\frac{1}{2}$ oz (75 g) butter, add 3 tablespoons flour and cook for a few minutes. Add the milk all at once and cook, stirring constantly, for about 5 minutes. Remove from heat and stir in 3 egg yolks, beaten with salt, pepper and paprika to taste, and 3 tablespoons grated Parmesan cheese. Leave to cool and fold in 3 egg whites, whipped until stiff. Pour mixture on the asparagus and bake in a hot oven (400°F/gas 6) for about 20 minutes or until risen and golden. Serve immediately.

Fish Soufflé

Melt 2 oz (60 g) butter in a pan, add 3 tablespoons flour and cook for a few minutes. Add $\frac{1}{2}$ pint ($\frac{1}{4}$ l) boiling milk all at once and cook, stirring constantly, for about 5 minutes. Remove from heat and stir in salt and pepper to taste, $2\frac{1}{2}$ oz (75 g) grated Gruyère cheese, 3 egg yolks, one at a time, and 3 oz (90 g) cold white fish, freshly cooked and shredded. Fold in 3 egg whites, beaten until stiff, and pour mixture into a buttered soufflé dish. Bake in a hot oven (400°F/gas 6) for 20 minutes, or until risen and golden. Serve immediately.

Brussels Sprouts Soufflé

Cook 1 lb (500 g) Brussels sprouts and $\frac{1}{2}$ lb (225 g) potatoes, peeled, in boiling salted water for 20 minutes, or until tender, then work through a sieve or food chopper. Add 3 egg yolks, 3 oz (90 g) butter and salt and pepper to taste, and beat until smooth. Fold in 3 egg whites, beaten until stiff, and pour into a soufflé dish. Sprinkle with grated Gruyère cheese and bake in a hot oven (350°F/gas 4) for 20 minutes. Serve immediately. Serves 6.

1

2

3

2

3

Cream Soups

Cream of Artichoke Soup

Ingredients: *4 large artichokes · lemon juice · $2\frac{1}{2}$ oz (75 g) butter · 2 oz (60 g) flour · $\frac{1}{2}$ pint ($\frac{1}{4}$ l) milk · salt · grated nutmeg · $1\frac{1}{4}$ pints ($\frac{3}{4}$ l) stock*

To finish: *parsley, finely chopped · bread croûtons, toasted or sautéed in butter until golden on all sides · grated cheese*

Clean the artichokes, halve them, discard the chokes and let stand in water with lemon juice to prevent discoloration. Cut in quarters and sauté over low heat in 1 oz (30 g) butter for 10–15 minutes (step 1). Prepare a béchamel sauce with the butter, flour, milk and salt and grated nutmeg to taste. Work the artichokes through a food chopper or sieve (step 2), add to the béchamel sauce and return pan to heat for 10 minutes. Add the stock and bring mixture to the boil. Add a generous amount of parsley. Serve with croûtons (step 3) and grated cheese.

Cream of Lentil Soup

Put 6 oz (175 g) dried lentils in cold water to cover with 1 clove of garlic, 1 carrot and 1 onion, all peeled, and a bouquet garni. Bring to the boil, skim off the scum and cook for about $1\frac{1}{2}$ hours. Remove and discard vegetables and bouquet garni and work lentils and their liquid through a food chopper or sieve. Prepare croûtons as for above recipe. Stir 1 oz (30 g) butter and 4 fl oz (100 ml) cream into the sieved lentils, reheat gently and serve immediately. Serve the croûtons separately.

Cream of Carrot Soup (Potage Crécy)

Put $\frac{1}{2}$ lb (225 g) carrots, peeled, 2 oz (60 g) rice, 1 onion, peeled, 1 bouquet garni, 1 leek, cleaned, and 1 quart (1 l) water in a pan. Bring to the boil and cook over low heat for about 45 minutes. Remove and discard the bouquet garni and work the mixture through a food chopper or sieve. Prepare croûtons as for above recipe. Stir 1 oz (30 g) butter and 4 fl oz (100 ml) cream into the sieved vegetables, reheat gently and serve immediately. Serve the croûtons separately.

1

2

3

Cream of Mushroom Soup

Ingredients: *¾ lb (350 g) fresh mushrooms or 2 tablespoons dried mushrooms, soaked in lukewarm water, squeezed dry and sliced · 2½ oz (75 g) butter · 1½ pints (¾ l) stock · 2 oz (60 g) flour · ½ pint (¼ l) milk · salt · grated nutmeg*

To finish: *parsley, chopped · croûtons*

Clean and trim fresh mushrooms (if using) and slice them finely (step 1). Heat 1 oz (30 g) butter in a small pan, add the mushrooms and sauté for a few minutes. Add some stock and cook, covered, over very low heat for about 15 minutes. Prepare a béchamel sauce with remaining butter, the flour, milk and salt and grated nutmeg to taste (step 2). Work mushrooms through a food chopper (step 3), add them to the béchamel sauce and cook for 10 minutes. Add remaining stock, bring to the boil and stir in the parsley. Serve with croûtons.

Cream of Pea Soup

Cover 10 oz (300 g) dried split peas with cold water and let stand for 1 hour. Drain, put in a pan with cold water to cover and a little salt and bring to the boil. Skim the scum from the surface, cover pan and cook over low heat for about ½ hour.

In another pan cook ½ onion, finely chopped, in 2 oz (60 g) butter until golden, add 1 carrot, peeled, the green part of 2 leeks, cleaned, a few chopped lettuce or spinach leaves and ¼ bay leaf and cook for a few minutes. Add the peas and their cooking water and cook, covered, over low heat for about 1 hour. Work through a food chopper or sieve and return to the heat and reheat gently. Add salt to taste, 2 oz (60 g) butter and a few tablespoons cream, if desired. Serve with 2 oz (60 g) diced ham, croûtons and a generous amount of grated Parmesan cheese.

Cream of Tomato Soup

Cook 1½ lb (750 g) tomatoes, peeled and chopped, 1 medium onion, sliced, ½ teaspoon sugar and a pinch of salt for ½ hour. Work the mixture through a food chopper or sieve and keep warm. In another pan heat 3 oz (90 g) butter, add 4 tablespoons flour and cook, stirring constantly, until well blended. Stir in 1 quart (1 l) cold milk and a pinch of salt and cook over low heat for about 20 minutes. Put a pinch of sodium bicarbonate in a soup tureen, pour in the tomato mixture and stir in the hot milk mixture. Mix well and serve with croûtons.

Potage Santé

Ingredients: *2–3 leeks, depending on size · $2\frac{1}{2}$ oz (75 g) butter · 1 lb (500 g) potatoes, peeled and quartered · water · salt · hot milk · $2\frac{1}{2}$ oz (75 g) sorrel leaves, chopped and cooked in 1 oz (30 g) butter · 1–2 egg yolks · a few tablespoons cream · $\frac{1}{2}$ teaspoon chervil*

To finish: *croûtons*

Slice the white parts of the leeks finely and cook in 1 oz (30 g) of the butter for a few minutes (step 1). Add the potatoes, $2\frac{1}{2}$ pints ($1\frac{1}{4}$ l) water and a little salt to taste, and cook until potatoes are tender. Work mixture through a food chopper or sieve (step 2), and thin the soup if necessary, with a little water and hot milk. Add the sorrel leaves and pour soup into a tureen (step 3). Stir in the egg yolks, mixed with the cream, the remaining butter and the chervil. Serve with fried or toasted croûtons in a separate dish.

Cream of Vegetable Soup

Clean and trim 1 small Savoy cabbage, slice finely, cover with boiling water and leave to stand. Finely slice 2 carrots, 2 potatoes, 1 turnip and the white part of 2 leeks, and cook over moderate heat in 1 oz (30 g) butter for a few minutes. Add $2\frac{1}{2}$ pints ($1\frac{1}{4}$ l) boiling stock and cook over low heat for 1 hour. Drain the cabbage and add to the mixture with 1 clove of garlic, peeled and crushed, and cook for 25 minutes. Work through a food chopper or sieve and add enough hot stock to obtain 1 quart (1 l) liquid. Reheat. Put 1 slice fried bread in each plate and pour the soup over.

Potage Dubarry

In a pan, cook 1 cauliflower, 1 onion, and 1 bay leaf in boiling salted water until cauliflower is tender.

Prepare a roux: in a small pan heat 2 oz (60 g) butter, add $1\frac{1}{2}$ oz (45 g) flour and cook mixture, stirring constantly, adding a few tablespoons cooking water from the cauliflower, until well blended and golden. Work the cauliflower and its cooking liquid through a food chopper or sieve, return to heat and stir in the roux, 2 egg yolks and 4 fl oz (100 ml) cream, without letting the mixture boil. Serve the soup immediately with crusty bread served separately.

Cream of Watercress Soup

Cook $\frac{3}{4}$ lb (350 g) potatoes, peeled, and 1 bunch watercress, washed and trimmed, in boiling salted water for $\frac{1}{2}$ hour. Work through a food chopper or sieve and add 2 oz (60 g) butter and 4 fl oz (100 ml) cream. Reheat gently and serve the soup immediately with croûtons in a separate dish.

1

2

3

1

2

3

Thick Soups

Zucchini and Tomato Soup

Ingredients: *4 zucchini · 1 or more tomatoes · 1 oz (30 g) butter · 1 clove of garlic, peeled · $2\frac{1}{2}$ pints ($1\frac{1}{4}$ l) stock · 4 oz (115 g) rice*

To finish: *grated Parmesan cheese*

Melt the butter in a large pan, add the garlic, cook for a few minutes then discard. Dice the zucchini (step 1) and sauté until golden (step 2). Chop the tomato and add to mixture. Cook for a few minutes, add the stock (step 3) and bring to the boil. Stir in rice and cook until *al dente*. Serve with grated Parmesan cheese.

Pistou

Wash 2 leeks, dry them and slice finely. Dip 4 tomatoes in boiling water and peel. Wash and peel 6 oz (175 g) potatoes and dice them. Put the leeks, 2 chopped tomatoes, the potatoes, 6 oz (175 g) green beans and 4 oz (115 g) kidney beans in a large pan with 2 quarts (2 l) water. Add salt and pepper to taste and cook for 15 minutes. Add 3 oz (90 g) vermicelli and cook for 15 minutes. Chop 3 cloves of garlic, the remaining 2 tomatoes and a generous amount of basil, and stir in 4 tablespoons olive oil and 2 oz (60 g) grated Gruyère cheese. Put garlic mixture in a soup tureen and pour in soup.

Leek and Rice Soup

Heat 2 oz (60 g) butter in a pan, add $\frac{3}{4}$ lb (350 g) leeks, washed, dried and thinly sliced, and cook for a few minutes. Add 1 teaspoon tomato paste and 3 pints ($1\frac{1}{2}$ l) stock and cook for about 20 minutes. Add 6 oz (175 g) rice and cook until rice is *al dente*. Add parsley, chopped, and serve with grated cheese.

Greek Vegetable Soup

Bring about $2\frac{1}{2}$ pints ($1\frac{1}{4}$ l) chicken stock to the boil, add about 6 oz (175 g) rice and cook until rice is *al dente*. In a soup tureen beat 2 egg yolks with the juice of 1 or 2 lemons and add 4 fl oz (100 ml) warm stock, stirring constantly. Add the rice and stock.

1

2

3

Minestrone Milanese

Ingredients: *1 oz (30 g) smoked bacon · 4 tablespoons olive oil · parsley, chopped · sage · 1 clove of garlic, peeled and finely chopped · 1 onion, finely chopped · a few celery sticks · 2 carrots · 1 leek · 1 tomato · 4 potatoes · fresh basil leaves, chopped · 6 oz (175 g) fresh beans, or dried beans soaked overnight in cold water and drained · 2 stock cubes · salt · pepper · ½ small Savoy cabbage, separated into leaves · 4 oz (115 g) rice or vermicelli*

To finish: *grated Parmesan cheese*

Chop and sauté the bacon, discarding liquid fat. In a large pan cook the oil, parsley to taste, sage, and the garlic and onion for a few minutes. Add the bacon, celery, carrots and leek, all finely sliced (step 1), the tomato, chopped, 2 potatoes, diced, and 2 whole potatoes (step 2), the basil and the beans (step 3). Cook for a few minutes, stirring constantly, add 5 pints (2½ l) hot, not boiling, water, the stock cubes, and salt and pepper to taste, and bring to the boil. Cook, covered, over low heat for 1¾ hours. Add the cabbage leaves and continue cooking for 45 minutes (in winter, cook cabbage for only 20 minutes). Add the rice 20 minutes before the end of the cooking time, or the vermicelli 8 minutes before the end of the cooking time, and serve with a generous amount of grated Parmesan cheese served separately.

Minestrone Genovese

Wash and chop 2 oz (60 g) carrots, 3 oz (90 g) zucchini, 10 oz (300 g) potatoes and 5 oz (150 g) Savoy cabbage. Place in a large pan with 1 tablespoon dried mushrooms, soaked in lukewarm water and squeezed dry, 6 oz (175 g) fresh peas, 3½ oz (100 g) dried beans, soaked overnight in cold water and drained, about 5 pints (2½ l) water, 1 oz (30 g) butter, salt and pepper and 2 stock cubes. Cook for 2 hours, then work through a food chopper or sieve. Return to heat and bring to the boil. Add 3 oz (90 g) fine vermicelli.

Five minutes before serving, blend in a chopped mixture of parsley, basil and garlic to taste, ½ oz (15 g) butter and 1½ tablespoons grated Parmesan cheese, all pounded together in a mortar.

Bean and Noodle Soup

Ingredients: *6 oz (175 g) dried red or kidney beans, soaked in cold water for 12 hours and drained • 2 oz (60 g) bacon fat, 1 celery stick, 1 small onion, 1 clove of garlic, parsley, basil, 3 oz (90 g) canned peeled tomatoes, all chopped • 2 quarts (2 l) cold water • 2 stock cubes • salt • pepper • 1 tablespoon oil • 6 oz (175 g) noodles*

Put the beans in a large pan (step 1), with the bacon fat, celery, onion, garlic, parsley, basil, tomatoes, and the water. Bring the mixture to the boil, add the stock cubes, salt and pepper to taste, and cook, covered, over low heat for about $1\frac{1}{2}$ hours. Work $\frac{1}{2}$ the beans through a sieve (step 2), and return to the pan. Raise the heat, add the noodles (step 3), and cook until noodles are *al dente*. Remove soup from the heat and let stand for a few minutes. Stir in the oil and serve immediately.

Potée Savoyarde

In a saucepan sauté 3 oz (90 g) chopped salt pork, for a few minutes, add 2 leeks and 1 onion, both sliced, and sauté for a few minutes. Add 1 celery stick and 10 oz (300 g) potatoes, peeled and sliced, and 1 quart (1 l) water and bring the mixture to the boil. Cook over medium heat for 30 minutes then stir in 1 pint ($\frac{1}{2}$ l) milk. Bring to the boil and cook over high heat for a few minutes, adding salt and pepper to taste. Grate 3 oz (90 g) Gruyère cheese, sprinkle on slices of crusty bread, and toast in the oven. Serve with the soup.

Brussels Sprouts Soup

Wash and trim 1 lb (500 g) Brussels sprouts and cook in boiling salted water with $\frac{1}{2}$ bay leaf, $\frac{1}{2}$ onion, thinly sliced, $\frac{1}{4}$ clove of garlic and a few parsley sprigs until tender. Drain and work through a food chopper. Add salt, pepper and grated nutmeg to taste, and 1 quart (1 l) stock, and bring to the boil. Serve with croûtons.

1

2

3

2

3

Onion Soup

Ingredients: *6 oz (175 g) onions, thinly sliced · 1½ oz (45 g) butter · 2 tablespoons flour · 2½ pints (1¼ l) stock · salt · pepper · bread · 2½ oz (75 g) grated Gruyère cheese*

Sauté the onions in the butter for a moment, sprinkle them with the flour (step 1) and, as soon as they start to brown, stir in the stock. Add salt and pepper to taste and cook for about 20 minutes. Place thin slices of bread in the bottom of a soup tureen, sprinkle with grated Gruyère cheese (step 2) and pour the soup over (step 3). Let stand for 10 minutes before serving, or sprinkle with more Gruyère cheese and put in a hot oven (400°F/gas 6) until golden and crusty on top.

Lentil Soup

Soak 1 lb (500 g) dried lentils in lukewarm water for 12 hours, drain and put in a pan with cold water to cover. Cook, covered for 2–3 hours, then work through a food chopper or sieve. In a small pan, heat 2 oz (60 g) butter, add a mixture of onion, celery, garlic and sage leaves, all chopped, and sauté for a few minutes. Stir the mixture into the lentils, add 2 stock cubes, salt and pepper to taste, and return the soup to the heat. Bring to the boil, remove from heat and serve with slices of bread fried in butter and a generous amount of grated Parmesan cheese.

Spinach Soup

Clean and wash 1½ lb (750 g) fresh spinach, cook without water and chop coarsely. Sauté quickly in 1 oz (30 g) butter and leave to cool. In a bowl beat 2 eggs with 2 tablespoons grated Parmesan cheese, and salt and grated nutmeg to taste, and stir into the spinach. Pour spinach into 2½ pints (1¼ l) boiling stock, return to heat and bring to the boil. Place 2 toasted bread slices in each plate, add soup and a generous amount of grated Parmesan cheese and serve immediately.

Auvergne Soup

In a large pan put 2 quarts (2 l) water, 4 carrots and 2 turnips, both sliced, one 2-lb (1-kg) cabbage, quartered, and 1 clove of garlic, peeled and crushed. Bring to the boil and simmer for about 10 minutes. Add 4 small potatoes, peeled and sliced, salt and pepper to taste, and cook for 10 minutes. Fry 3 oz (90 g) diced lean bacon in a frying pan, drain and add to the soup. Simmer for 5 minutes. Place a slice of French bread in each plate and pour the soup over them. Serves 6–8.

1

2

3

Broths and Consommés

Meat Consommé

Ingredients: *$\frac{3}{4}$ lb (350 g) stewing beef · $\frac{3}{4}$ lb (350 g) stewing veal · 1 beef bone · 1 veal knuckle · chicken neck and bones, if desired · $3\frac{1}{2}$ quarts ($3\frac{1}{2}$ l) water · salt · 3 peppercorns · 1 carrot, peeled · 1 onion, peeled and stuck with 1 clove · 1 bouquet garni of parsley and celery*

To clarify: *1 egg white*

Put the meats, bone and knuckle, and chicken neck and bones, if using, in a large pan with the water, salt and peppercorns, and bring very slowly to the boil, skimming the scum as it forms on the surface (step 1). Add the vegetables and bouquet garni (steps 2 and 3), and bring to the boil. Cook, covered, over low heat for 3 hours. Strain through a sieve, reserving the meats for other uses, and discard fat from surface, if soup is to be served immediately. (The broth can be left to stand until cold, and fat can then be removed from surface.)

To clarify: put 1 quart (1 l) cold broth in a pan with 1 egg white and bring to the boil, beating constantly with a wire whisk. Simmer, covered, over very low heat for $\frac{1}{2}$ hour and strain through a sieve covered with a cloth.

Chicken Consommé

Prepare a small chicken for cooking, slicing and reserving the heart and liver. If possible, brown it in the oven in a little butter. Place in a large pan with the reserved heart and liver, 3 quarts (3 l) water, and salt to taste. Bring slowly to the boil, skimming the scum as it forms on surface. Add 1 carrot, peeled, 1 leek, cleaned, and 1 small onion, quartered, and bring to the boil. Cook the chicken, covered, over low heat for $1\frac{1}{2}$–2 hours. Remove and discard vegetables and strain broth through a sieve covered with a cloth soaked in water and wrung dry. Serve very hot, preferably in small bowls or cups.

Cocky Leeky Soup

ngredients: *one 2-lb (1-kg) lean chicken · he white parts of 6 leeks, thinly sliced · 2 quarts (2 l) veal stock · 1 small carrot · 1 small onion, peeled · 1 celery stick · salt · 1$\frac{1}{2}$ oz (45 g) butter*

To serve: *16 prunes, cooked and pitted (optional)*

Put the chicken and stock in a pan and bring to he boil. Skim the scum as it forms on the surface, add the carrot, onion, celery, and salt o taste, and cook, covered, over low heat for about 1$\frac{1}{2}$ hours. Put chicken on a chopping board, remove and discard skin and bones and cut flesh into thin strips (step 1). Cook the leeks in the butter and a little salt (step 2). Remove fat from chicken broth and strain through a sieve. Return the chicken and leeks to the broth (step 3), and serve very hot. Prunes are traditionally served separately. Serves 4–6.

Mulligatawny Soup

Sauté one 2-lb (1-kg) chicken, cut into pieces, in 1 oz (30 g) butter until golden on all sides. Add 1 green apple, 1 green pepper and 1 carrot, all chopped, and cook for a few minutes. Sprinkle with 1 tablespoon flour, mixed with $\frac{1}{2}$ tablespoon curry powder, and stir in 3 quarts (3 l) hot water, a little at a time, $\frac{1}{2}$ tablespoon parsley, chopped, 1 clove, 1 pinch of pepper and $\frac{1}{2}$ tablespoon each of salt and sugar. Cover pan and cook over low heat for 1$\frac{1}{2}$ hours. Half an hour before the end of the cooking time, add 4 oz (115 g) tomatoes, worked through a food chopper or sieve, and continue cooking the mixture until chicken is tender. Remove the chicken from pan, discard skin and bones and cube the flesh. Strain the broth through a sieve and return the broth and chicken to the heat for a few minutes. Serve immediately in warm soup dishes, with boiled rice, in a separate dish.

2

3

3

Classic Consommé

Ingredients: *2 quarts (2 l) warm broth, prepared with beef, chicken and vegetables · ½ lb (225 g) lean beef · 1 small carrot and 1 leek, both thinly sliced · 1 egg white*

Clean the meat, removing all fat, and chop it. In a pan beat the meat and carrot, leek and egg white with a wire whisk (step 1). Beating constantly, add the broth a little at a time (step 2). Bring the mixture slowly to the boil, stirring constantly, and cook, covered, over very low heat for about 1 hour. Strain through a fine cloth, soaked in lukewarm water and wrung dry (step 3), then bring to the boil. The consommé should be perfectly clear. Serve in small bowls or cups.

Consommé Fantasia

Beat 3 eggs with a little salt until light and foamy, and stir in a generous handful of fresh spinach, chopped, 1 oz (30 g) Italian prosciutto, chopped, and 2 tablespoons grated Parmesan cheese. Cook the mixture on both sides as you would a frittata and cut it into thin strips. Divide the strips equally between 4 bowls or cups and pour in boiling consommé. Serve immediately.

Chicken Consommé with Marsala

Prepare chicken broth, leave to cool and remove the fat from the surface. Return to the heat, stir in 1 egg white and bring to the boil, beating constantly with a wire whisk. Strain the consommé through 2 or 3 fine cloths or through cheesecloth. Return to the heat, stir in 1 glass dry Marsala for each quart (litre) of consommé, and bring to the boil. Serve immediately in small bowls or cups.

nocchetti in Broth

ngredients: *1 oz (30 g) butter, at room emperature · $3\frac{1}{2}$ tablespoons grated Parmesan heese · 2 eggs, separated · salt · grated utmeg · $3\frac{1}{2}$ oz (100 g) semolina · $2\frac{1}{2}$ pints $1\frac{1}{4}$ l) broth*

n a bowl beat the butter with the Parmesan heese. Add the egg yolks, beating constantly, nd salt and nutmeg to taste. Beat the egg vhite with a wire whisk until stiff (step 1) and old into mixture with a metal spoon. Add the emolina (step 2). Bring the broth to the boil, lrop in the semolina mixture, a teaspoon at a ime (step 3), and cook for about 15 minutes.

.iver Gnocchetti for onsommés and Broths

hop 6 oz (175 g) veal liver very finely or work t through the finest blade of a food chopper. In frying pan sauté 1 slice onion and a little parsey, both finely chopped, in 2 oz (60 g) butter or a few minutes. Add the liver and 2 oz (60 g) vhite bread, soaked in milk and squeezed dry, nd cook the mixture over moderate heat for a ew minutes, stirring constantly. Let stand until ool, stir in 2 eggs, 4 tablespoons breadcrumbs, little grated nutmeg, and salt to taste, and et stand for $\frac{1}{2}$ hour.

With floured fingers, form walnut-sized alls and cook them in about $2\frac{1}{2}$ pints ($1\frac{1}{4}$ l) roth for 20 minutes. Serve immediately in varm soup dishes.

hicken Gnocchetti for onsommés and Broths

ook 4 oz (115 g) potatoes in boiling salted water until tender, drain, peel and put through a otato ricer or work them through a sieve. tir in $\frac{1}{2}$ chicken breast, cooked until tender in little water and finely chopped, 2 tablespoons grated Parmesan cheese, 2 egg yolks, 2 tablespoons flour, salt and grated nutmeg to taste, nd mix well. On a floured board form the nixture into small finger shapes and cut them nto thick slices. Cook the gnocchetti in $2\frac{1}{2}$ pints $1\frac{1}{4}$ l) boiling broth for 6–8 minutes. Serve mmediately in warm soup dishes, with grated armesan cheese.

2

3

1

2

3

Passatelli in Bouillon

Ingredients: *4 tablespoons breadcrumbs · 2 eggs · 2 tablespoons grated Parmesan cheese · 1 tablespoon flour · $\frac{3}{4}$ oz (22 g) beef marrow · salt · pepper · nutmeg · $2\frac{1}{2}$ pints ($1\frac{1}{4}$ l) boiling broth*

To serve: *grated Parmesan cheese*

In a bowl blend the breadcrumbs together with the eggs, Parmesan cheese, flour, beef marrow, and salt, pepper and grated nutmeg to taste, until mixture is smooth (step 1). Work the paste carefully through a passatelli machine (step 2), a food chopper, using the blade with the largest holes, or a potato ricer. As the passatelli form, scrape them with the blade of a knife into the boiling broth (step 3). Cook gently over low heat for 5 minutes, pour into warm soup dishes and serve with grated Parmesan cheese in a separate dish.

Gnocchetti Bolognese

Melt 2 oz (60 g) butter over low heat without letting it brown; leave to cool. Stir in $3\frac{1}{2}$ tablespoons flour, 1 egg, 3 tablespoons grated Parmesan cheese, salt and grated nutmeg to taste, and spread the mixture on a plate. Bring $2\frac{1}{2}$ pints ($1\frac{1}{4}$ l) stock to the boil and, using 2 teaspoons dipped occasionally in the boiling stock, drop mixture by spoonfuls into the stock. Cook over moderate heat for 3–4 minutes, and serve with grated Parmesan cheese.

Soup in a Bag

In a bowl beat 3 eggs and stir in 6 tablespoons flour, 5 tablespoons grated Parmesan cheese, 3 oz (90 g) butter, melted, salt to taste and a little grated nutmeg. With floured fingers, shape mixture into a ball and place in the middle of a damp cloth or in a cotton bag, tying firmly with string. Put bag in 3 pints ($1\frac{1}{2}$ l) boiling broth and cook for 40 minutes. Remove bag from broth and let cool. Remove mixture from bag, cut into slices and then into cubes. Return cubes to broth and cook for 8 minutes. Serve with grated Parmesan cheese.

Stracciatella

Bring $2\frac{1}{2}$ pints ($1\frac{1}{4}$ l) stock to the boil. In a bowl beat 4 eggs with 2 teaspoons breadcrumbs, 4 tablespoons grated Parmesan cheese, a little parsley, chopped, salt and grated nutmeg to taste. Add 2 tablespoons water or cold broth, pour the mixture into boiling broth and cook over moderate heat for 3–4 minutes, stirring constantly with a wire whisk. Serve with grated Parmesan cheese.

Profiteroles for Consommé

Ingredients: *2 fl oz (50 ml) water · ½ oz (15 g) butter · 1½ oz (45 g) flour · 1 egg*

In a small pan bring the water, butter and a pinch of salt to the boil, remove the pan from the heat and pour the flour in all at once. Stir the mixture until well blended, then return to the heat for 3–4 minutes, stirring constantly. Leave to cool, stir in the egg (step 1), and beat vigorously until the dough is light. Using a pastry bag fitted with a large tube (step 2), pipe the dough into walnut-sized balls on a lightly damp baking sheet (step 3), leaving some space between each ball. Cook the profiteroles in a hot oven (400°F/gas 6) for about 15 minutes or until they are puffed and golden. Do not open the oven door during the cooking time. Serve with boiling consommé in a separate dish.

Julienne for Consommé

Clean and wash 1 onion, 1 carrot, 1 leek, 1 celery stick or other vegetables to taste and cut them into thin strips. Cook in 1 oz (30 g) butter for a few minutes, add a little salt and some broth and cook, covered, over low heat until they are *al dente*. Drain the vegetables, put them in a soup tureen or in individual bowls or cups, pour in boiling consommé and serve the soup with grated Parmesan cheese in a separate dish.

Royale for Consommé

Beat 2 eggs vigorously and slowly stir in ½ pint (¼ l) chicken broth, 1 tablespoon asparagus purée, 1 tablespoon pea purée, salt and pepper to taste. Pour the mixture in a buttered bowl and cook in a bain-marie or in the top of a double boiler for 20–25 minutes or until set. Remove from the heat and leave to cool. Cut the royale into cubes or other shapes to taste. Pour boiling consommé over the cubes and serve the soup immediately.

2

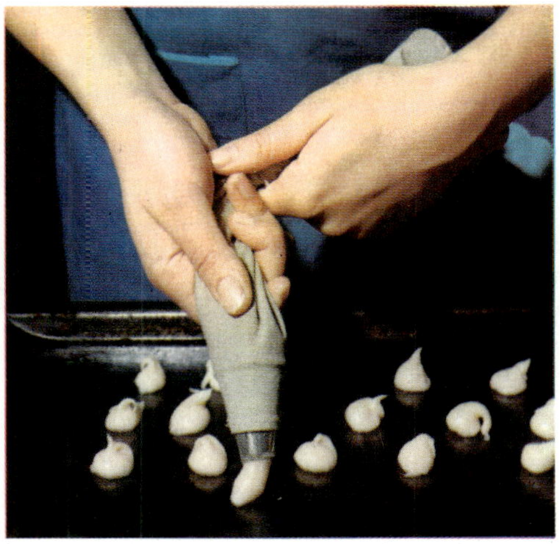

3

1

2

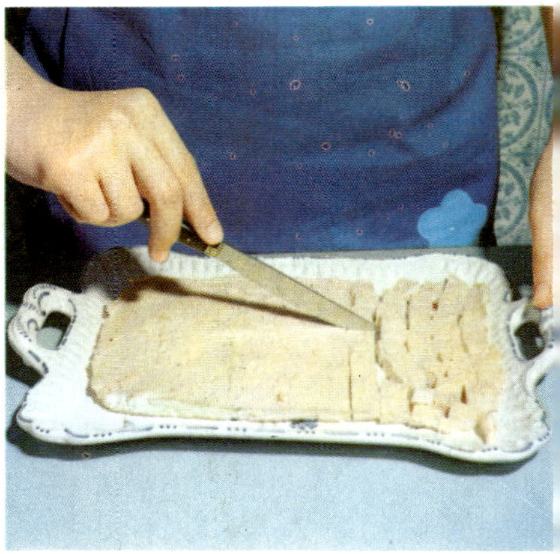

3

Calabrian Consommé

Ingredients: *6 oz (175 g) ricotta or other white cheese · 4 tablespoons grated Parmesan cheese · 2 eggs, separated · salt · pepper · grated nutmeg · 1 quart (1 l) boiling consommé*

Work the ricotta through a sieve into a bowl and stir in half the Parmesan cheese, the egg yolks, salt, pepper and grated nutmeg to taste. Beat egg whites until stiff and, with a metal spoon, fold into mixture (step 1). Butter an ovenproof rectangular mould and line it with buttered wax paper. Pour the mixture into the mould (step 2), and cook in a bain-marie in a moderate oven (350°F/gas 4) until set and golden on top. Remove the mould from the oven and leave to cool. Remove the wax paper carefully and cut the cheese mixture into small cubes (step 3). Put the cubes into individual soup plates, pour in boiling consommé and serve immediately with the remaining grated Parmesan cheese.

Cold Jellied Consommé

Cook 1 lb (500 g) tomatoes, peeled and quartered, and 1 celery stick in 3 quarts (3 l) consommé for 1 hour. Work the consommé through a sieve lined with a thin cloth and leave to cool. Refrigerate until lightly set, putting very thin sheets of paper on the surface to remove the fat rising to the surface. Serve the consommé in individual bowls or cups with a small sprig of parsley and a thin slice of lemon in each. Serves 12.

Consommé Celestine

In a bowl blend 2 eggs with 5 oz (150 g) flour and $\frac{1}{2}$ teaspoon salt. Stir in $\frac{1}{2}$ pint ($\frac{1}{4}$ l) milk, a little at a time, $\frac{1}{2}$ oz (15 g) butter, lightly melted, and 1 tablespoon parsley, chopped. Beat the batter with a wire whisk until smooth. Heat 2 oz (60 g) butter in a small frying pan. Pour in 1 tablespoon batter and quickly tilt and rotate the pan so that the bottom is thinly and evenly coated. Cook the crêpe until the bottom is golden, flip it over and finish cooking. Continue in this manner until all the batter is used. Roll up the crêpes and slice thinly. Pour boiling consommé over the strips and serve immediately with grated Parmesan cheese.